Teacher Guide

Perfection Learning®

Acknowledgments

Excerpt from *Warrior Lessons* by Phoebe Eng. Copyright © 1999 by Phoebe Eng. Reprinted by permission of Simon & Schuster Inc.

Excerpt from *Nelson Mandela: No Easy Walk to Freedom* by Barry Denenberg. Copyright © 1991 by Barry Denenberg. Reprinted by permission of Scholastic, Inc.

Excerpts from *Falling Leaves: The True Story of an Unwanted Chinese Daughter* by Adeline Yen Mah. Copyright © 1997 by Adeline Yen Mah. Reprinted by permission of John Wiley & Sons, Inc.

Excerpt from *Black Ice* by Lorene Cary. Copyright © 1991 by Lorene Cary. Used by permission of Alfred A. Knopf, a division of Random House, Inc.

Excerpt from *Reason for Hope: A Spiritual Journey* by Jane Goodall and Phillip Berman.

Perfection Learning®

Printed in the United States of America. For information, contact Perfection Learning® Corporation, 1000 North Second Avenue, P.O. Box 500, Logan, Iowa 51546-0500.
Tel: 1-800-831-4190 • Fax: 1-800-543-2745
perfectionlearning.com

Paperback ISBN 0-7891-5656-3
3 4 5 6 7 8 PP 08 07 06 05 04

Table of Contents

Using the *Vocabu-Lit* Program

Vocabu-Lit is a unique lit-based program designed to help your students improve their word power. In format and approach, it differs in several ways from the usual vocabulary-building materials.

First, *Vocabu-Lit* contains examples of how the vocabulary words have been used by various writers and speakers. The inclusion of classic and high-interest literature not only will interest students in good writing but also will show them how vocabulary can become an effective writing tool.

Second, *Vocabu-Lit* does not ask students to learn a large number of words at one sitting. Instead, students master just ten words at a time and are provided several experiences with those words. Each experience reinforces the previous one, helping students to master meaning.

Third, *Vocabu-Lit* capitalizes on students' natural approach to language acquisition by having them study words in context. Learning words through context aids students in two ways. First, it leads them to define a word more precisely. It also helps them develop an important reading skill: the ability to discover and use contextual clues to determine meaning.

Reading the Passage

Each lesson begins with a selection from a book, essay, story, poem, or speech. Students are encouraged to read straight through the selection without paying particular attention to the Master Words (the ten words in dark type). Their understanding of the general meaning of the passage should help them determine the definitions of the Master Words. Students are advised to read the passage again, this time paying closer attention to the Master Words.

Self-testing for Understanding

The first exercise is a self-test designed to help students identify the words that they have not yet mastered. Often students will think they know a Master Word only to find that the contextual meaning of the word differs from their own understanding of its meaning. Or they may be unable to state the exact definition. This exercise teaches students to examine a word in context and define its meaning more precisely.

Sometimes the word is actually defined by context. For example, "He was *mendicant* because he had to beg." Other times, opposite or contrasting terms reveal the word's meaning: "He was far from poor; in fact, he was *affluent*." Sometimes an unfamiliar word may be followed by examples that explain it, as in "Mrs. Murphy was a *hospitable* woman who warmly welcomed her son's friends." From the context, which in this case consists of an example, the students should have little difficulty figuring out that *hospitable* means "giving a friendly welcome to guests." Selections may also include key words such as *means, is, for example, in other words,* or *and so forth.* All of these are clues that help the students determine a word's meaning.

Note: In some cases, the form of the Master Word in the self-test is not the same as in the passage. Generally, these changes were made to provide students with a more commonly used form of the word.

Writing Definitions

In the second exercise, students are asked to write definitions of the Master Words. The first part of the exercise asks that they define as many of the ten words as they can without using a dictionary. Students should use context clues and any previous experience with the words to write their definitions.

The second part of the exercise asks that the students consult a dictionary and copy an appropriate definition for each word in the space provided. A reproducible glossary is provided in the back of this teacher's guide should you wish to substitute it for a dictionary.

Note: The part of speech of the words as they will be used in the *exercises* is already indicated in the exercise. This may be different from the words' function in the passage, but students may still find contextual clues helpful.

Choosing Synonyms and Antonyms

In this exercise, students pick a synonym and antonym for each Master Word. Before students begin the lesson, you may wish to review the meanings of *synonym* and *antonym*.

Since students may not be familiar with all the words in the list of synonyms and antonyms, they may find it useful to keep dictionaries handy.

Note: There are no appropriate antonyms for some Master Words. In such cases, the antonym blank has been marked with an X. Also, a synonym or antonym may seem to match more than one Master Word in the exercise. Both possible answers are indicated in the teacher guide.

Completing Analogies

In the forth exercise, students complete word analogies using the Master Words. Again, students will be working with synonyms and antonyms (though different from those in the third exercise).

Before attempting to complete this activity, students should be shown how to read analogies. Try introducing them to the concept with the following example.

day :night ::rich : __________

Tell students that the symbol : means "is to" and :: means "as." Thus, the analogy could be read "Day is to night as rich is to __________."

Point out to students that the words *day* and *night* are opposites, or antonyms. So they should look for an antonym of *rich* in their list of Master Words. The Master Word *penniless* would be a correct response.

Fitting Words into Context

The next exercise includes ten sentences, which students complete with the appropriate Master Words. Each sentence supplies clues to help students select the best answer. Thus, while testing understanding of the new words, this exercise also provides another contextual setting for the Master Words.

Playing with the Words

In the final exercise, students use the Master Words to solve a variety of puzzles. Traditional games such as acrostics, crosswords, and word spirals are offered. But there are also more novel puzzles that challenge students to complete play associations and word fact tables, to arrange words by degree, and to invent definitions for portmanteau (or merged) Master Words. They are even invited to write stories using some of their newly acquired vocabulary.

Reviewing Knowledge

There are three review lessons in every *Vocabu-Lit* (Lessons 12, 24, and 36). Students test their mastery of the vocabulary words from the previous eleven lessons by completing sentences and analogies.

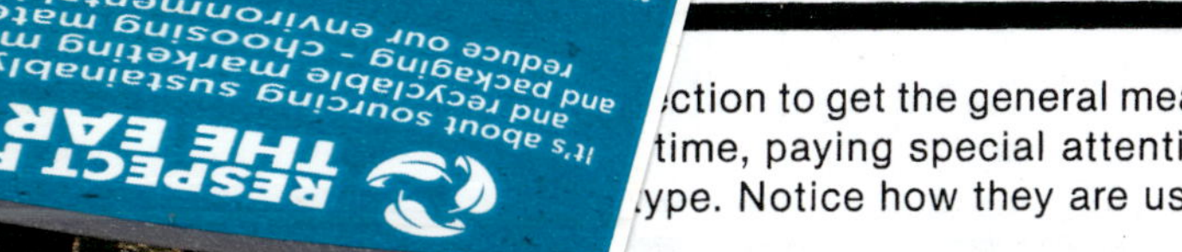

[illegible] ction to get the general meaning [illegible] time, paying special attention [illegible] ype. Notice how they are used in sentences. These are Master Words. These are the words you will be working with in this lesson.

[illegible] ph, Cupid, and the Clock''

[illegible] s strayed dreamily through the [illegible] Michael, as he smiled under the [illegible] **polychromatic** beard. Lounging [illegible] the poorest of **mendicants** in the [illegible] ved to study **humanity**. He found in **altr**[illegible] more pleasure than his riches, his station and all the grosser sweets of life had given him. It was his chief **solace** and satisfaction to **alleviate** individual distress, to confer favors upon worthy ones who had need of **succor**, to dazzle unfortunates by unexpected and bewildering gifts of truly royal magnificence, **bestowed**, however, with wisdom and judiciousness.

And as Prince Michael's eye rested upon the glowing face of the great clock in the tower, his smile, altruistic as it was, became slightly tinged with contempt. Big thoughts were the Prince's; and it was always with a shake of his head that he considered the **subjugation** of the world to the arbitrary measures of Time. The comings and goings of people in hurry and dread, controlled by the little metal moving hands of a clock, always made him sad.

By and by came a young man in evening clothes and sat upon the third bench from the Prince. For half an hour he smoked cigars with nervous haste, and then he fell to watching the face of the illuminated clock above the trees. His **perturbation** was evident, and the Prince noted, in sorrow, that its cause was connected, in some manner, with the slowly moving hands of the timepiece.

EXERCISE 1

SELF-TEST: After reading the above selection, do the following. Look at the Master Words below. Underline the words that you think you know. Circle the words that you are less sure about. Draw a square around the words you don't recognize.

MASTER WORDS

alleviate	**perturbation**
altruism	**polychromatic**
bestow	**solace**
humanity	**subjugation**
mendicant	**succor**

EXERCISE 2

Read the selection on the preceding page again, this time paying special attention to the ten Master Words. In the (a) spaces provided below, write down what you think is the meaning of the word. After you have attempted a definition for each word, look up the word in a dictionary. In the (b) spaces, copy the appropriate dictionary definition.

1. **alleviate** (v.)
   a. ______
   b. to make less severe; to lighten as a burden; to remove stress
2. **altruism** (n.)
   a. ______
   b. unselfish consideration for others; selflessness
3. **bestow** (v.)
   a. ______
   b. to give; to apply; also, to use
4. **humanity** (n.)
   a. ______
   b. humankind; all humans collectively
5. **mendicant** (n.)
   a. ______
   b. beggar; one who asks for charity
6. **perturbation** (n.)
   a. ______
   b. disquiet; state of being disturbed or confused
7. **polychromatic** (adj.)
   a. ______
   b. multicolored; many-hued; dazzling
8. **solace** (n.)
   a. ______
   b. relief from grief or anxiety; state of comfort
9. **subjugation** (n.)
   a. ______
   b. condition of being under the power of another; lack of freedom
10. **succor** (n.)
    a. ______
    b. help; relief; aid

EXERCISE 3

Use the following list of synonyms and antonyms to fill in the blanks. Some words have no antonyms. In such cases, the antonym blanks have been marked with an X.

animals	defiance	financier	self-centeredness
beggar	deprive	give	serenity
colorless	distraction	intensify	subservience
comfort	distress	neglect	unselfishness
compassion	ease	people	vivid

	Synonyms	Antonyms
1. **polychromatic**	(vivid)	(colorless)
2. **mendicant**	(beggar)	(financier)
3. **humanity**	(people)	(animals)
4. **altruism**	(unselfishness)	(self-centeredness)
5. **solace**	(comfort)	(distress)
6. **alleviate**	(ease)	(intensify)
7. **succor**	(compassion)	(neglect)
8. **bestow**	(give)	(deprive)
9. **subjugation**	(subservience)	(defiance)
10. **perturbation**	(distraction)	(serenity) (comfort)

EXERCISE 4

Decide whether the first pair in the items below are synonyms or antonyms. Then choose the Master Word that shows a similar relation to the word(s) preceding the blank.

1. intellectual	:reasoning	::humankind	: (humanity)
2. peculiarity	:oddity	::colorful	: (polychromatic)
3. import	:value	::charity case	: (mendicant)
4. inspire	:discourage	::independence	: (subjugation)
5. abrupt	:steady	::grief	: (solace) (succor)
6. minute	:gigantic	::harm	: (succor) (solace)
7. suspend	:proceed	::calmness	: (perturbation)
8. frail	:fragile	::kindness	: (altruism)
9. anticipate	:foresee	::present	: (bestow)
10. egotism	:meekness	::worsen	: (alleviate)

EXERCISE 5

The Master Words in this lesson are repeated below. From the Master Words, choose the appropriate word for the blank in each of the following sentences. Write the word in the numbered space provided at the right.

alleviate	bestow	mendicant	polychromatic	subjugation
altruism	humanity	perturbation	solace	succor

1. He registered little ...?... at the sharp questioning from the prosecuting attorney. 1. (perturbation)
2. Aspirin does not get at causes but it may help ...?... pain temporarily. 2. (alleviate)
3. The ...?... of minorities is one characteristic of fascism. 3. (subjugation)
4. Although it may be cold comfort, defeated politicians can find some ...?... in that they have tried what others talk about. 4. (solace) (succor)
5. It is customary to ...?... best wishes on newlyweds. 5. (bestow)
6. A school classroom should be ...?... rather than the usual simple brown tone. 6. (polychromatic)
7. Acts that are individually kind extend to all ...?... as well. 7. (humanity)
8. Although cynics may not believe it, some people do act from ...?... rather than personal glorification. 8. (altruism)
9. Knights of old in trouble occasionally sought ...?... even from their enemies. 9. (succor) (solace)
10. On Skid Row, a tourist may be stopped by (a, an) ...?... carrying a sign saying, "Loose change for a meal." 10. (mendicant)

EXERCISE 6

Write the Master Word that is associated with each word group below.

1. saint, Nobel Prize, Gandhi (altruism)
2. high blood pressure, stress, nervousness (perturbation)
3. Red Cross, Peace Corps, Good Samaritan (succor)
4. inheritance, award, citizenship (bestow)
5. dictator, prisoner of war, slave (subjugation)
6. rainbow, bouquet, kaleidoscope (polychromatic)
7. sympathy card, friend, security blanket (solace)
8. panhandler, alms, street musician (mendicant)
9. Novocain, aspirin, heating pad (alleviate)
10. community, masses, Homo sapiens (humanity)

LESSON 2

Read the following selection to get the general meaning. Read it a second time, paying special attention to the words in dark type. Notice how they are used in sentences. These are Master Words. These are the words you will be working with in this section.

from ***Warrior Lessons: An Asian American Woman's Journey into Power***
by Phoebe Eng

In the 1970s, in the Long Island suburb where we lived, **multiculturalism** and **diversity** were pretty simple **concepts**. The **motto** was simple and basic: "Do whatever you can to be like everyone else, and you'll be absolutely fine." As in most suburban **enclaves** then and even now, "belonging" was the goal, and that meant differences had to be hidden at any cost, no matter how **patent** and **indelible** those differences might be. Deny your differences and they won't exist, my father would tell us back then. "You're just as American as anybody else," he'd say. And in enlightened times, perhaps he'd have been right. But back in the seventies it didn't explain why we were called Chinks or why parents voiced polite concern at a PTA meeting when I was given the female lead in our high school bicentennial production of *Oklahoma!*, implying that Asian Americanness was actually unAmerican.

I thought the rest of America, like my own town, was Jewish, and so Jewish is what I aspired to become. Our family must have been good at the assimilation game, since we were eventually jokingly **dubbed** the "Engsteins," a term of **endearment** and acceptance that must have meant: You are an **honorary** one of us. And because of this we do not notice your differences (really, we swear!). Even if we don't always understand you mom's heavy Chinese accent.

EXERCISE 1

SELF-TEST: After reading the above selection, do the following. Look at the Master Words below. Underline the words that you think you know. Circle the words that you are less sure about. Draw a square around the words you don't recognize.

MASTER WORDS	
concepts	**honorary**
diversity	**indelible**
dubbed	**motto**
enclaves	**multiculturalism**
endearment	**patent**

EXERCISE 2

Read the following selection to get the general meaning. Read it a second time, paying special attention to the words in dark type. Notice how they are used in sentences. These are Master Words. These are the words you will be working with in this section.

1. **concepts** (n.)

   a. __________

   b. ideas; things conceived in the mind

2. **diversity** (n.)

   a. __________

   b. quality or state of having different forms or types

3. **dubbed** (v.)

   a. __________

   b. named or called

4. **enclaves** (n.)

   a. __________

   b. distinct territorial, cultural, or social units

5. **endearment** (n.)

   a. __________

   b. word or act expressing affection

6. **honorary** (adj.)

   a. __________

   b. conferred in recognition of achievement or service without the usual obligations

7. **indelible** (adj.)

   a. __________

   b. permanent; that which cannot be washed away or erased

8. **motto** (n.)

   a. __________

   b. short expression of a guiding principle

9. **multiculturalism** (n.)

   a. __________

   b. relating to, reflecting, or adapted to diverse cultures

10. **patent** (adj.)

   a. __________

   b. obvious; readily visible or intelligible

EXERCISE 3

Read the following selection to get the general meaning. Read it a second time, paying special attention to the words in dark type. Notice how they are used in sentences. These are Master Words. These are the words you will be working with in this section.

affection	ideas	permanent	uniformity
complimentary	neighborhoods	questionable	variety
estrangement	nicknamed	slogan	various cultures
homogeneity	obvious	transient	

	Synonyms	Antonyms
1. **multiculturalism**	(various cultures)	(homogeneity or uniformity)
2. **diversity**	(variety)	(uniformity or homogeneity)
3. **concepts**	(ideas)	X
4. **motto**	(slogan)	X
5. **enclaves**	(neighborhoods)	X
6. **patent**	(obvious)	(questionable)
7. **indelible**	(permanent)	(transient)
8. **dubbed**	(nicknamed)	X
9. **endearment**	(affection)	(estrangement)
10. **honorary**	(complimentary)	X

EXERCISE 4

Decide whether the first pair in the items below are synonyms or antonyms. Then choose the Master Word that shows a similar relation to the word(s) preceding the blank.

1. pact	:agreement	::slogan	: (motto)
2. concave	:convex	::estrangement	: (endearment)
3. approach	:withdraw	::uniformity	: (diversity)
4. imperial	:majestic	::named	: (dubbed)
5. control	:dominion	::thoughts	: (concepts)
6. decisive	:tentative	::questionable	: (patent)
7. evasive	:vague	::various cultures	: (multiculturalism)
8. frightening	:ominous	::neighborhoods	: (enclaves)
9. careless	:negligent	::complimentary	: (honorary)
10. income	:expense	::transient	: (indelible)

EXERCISE 5

The Master Words in this lesson are repeated below. From the Master Words, choose the appropriate word for the blank in each of the following sentences. Write the word in the numbered space provided at the right.

concepts	dubbed	endearment	inedlible	multiculturalism
diversity	enclaves	honorary	motto	patent

1. The evidence of his guilt was so ...?... as to be laughable. 1. (patent)
2. We were amazed at the ...?... of birds in so small an area. 2. (diversity)
3. Chicago still has many ethnic ...?..., made up of recent and not-so-recent immigrants. 3. (enclaves)
4. His mother messed up his hair in a gesture of ...?... . 4. (endearment)
5. As she listened, she realized she had never been exposed to such strange and wonderful ...?... before. 5. (concepts)
6. The holiday festival featured so many ethnic traditions that it seemed an exercise in ...?... . 6. (multiculturalism)
7. He looked frantically for a way to remove the ...?... ink from the pocket of his shirt. 7. (indelible)
8. The school needed a new ...?... that would convey its new sense of spirit. 8. (motto)
9. It was only (a, an) ...?... degree, but it made the family swell with pride just the same. 9. (honorary)
10. Because of his clumsiness, he was ...?... "Sir Grace." 10. (dubbed)

EXERCISE 6

Complete the wordsearch puzzle.

concepts
diversity
dubbed
enclaves
endearment
honorary
indelible
motto
multicultural
patent

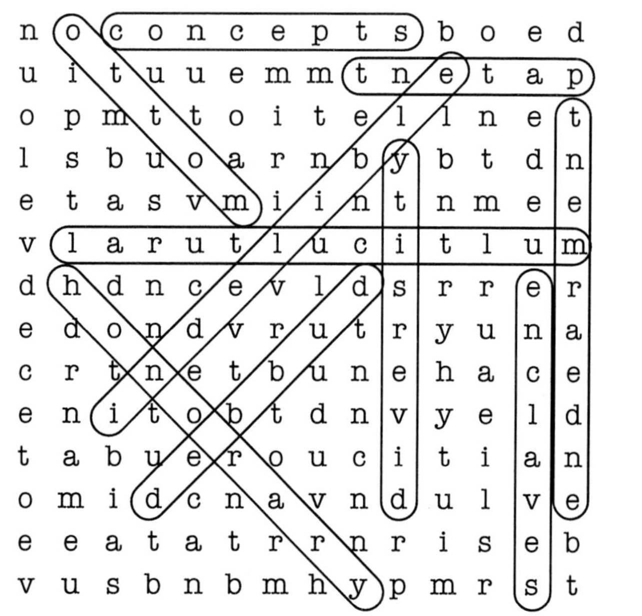

LESSON 3

Read the following selection to get the general meaning. Read it a second time, paying special attention to the words in dark type. Notice how they are used in sentences. These are Master Words. These are the words you will be working with in this lesson.

From **The Yosemite**
by John Muir

The Nevada Fall is 600 feet high and is usually ranked next to the Yosemite in general interest among the five main falls of the Valley. Coming through the Little Yosemite in **tranquil** reaches, the river is first broken into rapids on a moraine boulder-bar that crosses the lower end of the Valley. Then it pursues its way to the head of the fall in a rough, solid rock channel, dashing on side angles, heaving in heavy surging masses against elbow knobs, and swirling and swashing in potholes without a moment's rest. Thus, already **chafed** and dashed to foam, overfolded and twisted, it plunges over the brink of the precipice as if glad to escape into the open air. But before it reaches the bottom it is **pulverized** yet finer by **impinging** upon a sloping portion of the cliff about half-way down, thus making it the whitest of all the falls of the Valley, and altogether one of the most wonderful in the world. . . .

The Vernal, about a mile below the Nevada, is 400 feet high, a **staid**, orderly, graceful, easy-going fall, proper and exact in every movement and gesture, with scarce a hint of the passionate enthusiasm of the Yosemite or of the **impetuous** Nevada, whose chafed and twisted waters hurrying over the cliff seem glad to escape into the open air, while its deep, booming thunder-tones **reverberate** over the listening landscape. Nevertheless it is a favorite with most visitors, doubtless because it is more **accessible** than any other, more closely approached and better seen and heard. A good stairway **ascends** the cliff beside it and the level plateau at the head enables one to **saunter** safely along the edge of the river as it comes from Emerald Pool. . . .

EXERCISE 1

SELF-TEST: After reading the above selection, do the following. Look at the Master Words below. Underline the words that you think you know. Circle the words that you are less sure about. Draw a square around the words you don't recognize.

MASTER WORDS

accessible	**pulverize**
ascend	**reverberate**
chafe	**saunter**
impetuous	**staid**
impinge	**tranquil**

EXERCISE 2

Read the selection on the preceding page again, this time paying special attention to the ten Master Words. In the (a) spaces provided below, write down what you think is the meaning of the word. After you have attempted a definition for each word, look up the word in a dictionary. In the (b) spaces, copy the appropriate dictionary definition.

1. **accessible** (adj.)
   a. ______
   b. open to approach; easily reached
2. **ascend** (v.)
   a. ______
   b. to move from lower to higher position; to rise
3. **chafe** (v.)
   a. ______
   b. to rub; to irritate by rubbing; to heat by friction
4. **impetuous** (adj.)
   a. ______
   b. acting with sudden energy, sometimes without thought; rushing with force
5. **impinge** (v.)
   a. ______
   b. to encroach or invade; to collide; to infringe upon
6. **pulverize** (v.)
   a. ______
   b. to reduce to fine powder; to disintegrate; to smash
7. **reverberate** (v.)
   a. ______
   b. to echo; to resound, like a series of echoes
8. **saunter** (v.)
   a. ______
   b. to walk idly with no special concern; to amble
9. **staid** (adj.)
   a. ______
   b. serious; sober
10. **tranquil** (adj.)
    a. ______
    b. peaceful; serene; quiet; undisturbed

EXERCISE 3

Use the following list of synonyms and antonyms to fill in the blanks. Some words have no antonyms. In such cases, the antonym blanks have been marked with an X.

agitated	caress	echo	silence
amble	climb	impulsive	sink
attainable	cloistered	restrained	solidify
avoid	collide	rub	stride
calm	demolish	sedate	wild

	Synonyms	Antonyms
1. **tranquil**	(calm)	(agitated)
2. **chafe**	(rub)	(caress)
3. **pulverize**	(demolish)	(solidify)
4. **impinge**	(collide)	(avoid)
5. **staid**	(sedate) (restrained)	(wild)
6. **impetuous**	(impulsive)	(restrained) (sedate)
7. **reverberate**	(echo)	(silence)
8. **accessible**	(attainable)	(cloistered)
9. **ascend**	(climb)	(sink)
10. **saunter**	(amble)	(stride)

EXERCISE 4

Decide whether the first pair in the items below are synonyms or antonyms. Then choose the Master Word that shows a similar relation to the word(s) preceding the blank.

1. festooned	:plain	::remote	: (accessible)
2. invincible	:unprotected	::plunge	: (ascend)
3. tortuous	:winding	::crush	: (pulverize)
4. somber	:sunny	::cautious	: (impetuous)
5. maze	:tangle	::stroll	: (saunter)
6. prow	:nose	::serious	: (staid)
7. lair	:hideout	::resound	: (reverberate)
8. tracery	:lacework	::irritate	: (chafe)
9. distorted	:distinct	::unsettled	: (tranquil)
10. ooze	:stream	::back off	: (impinge)

EXERCISE 5

The Master Words in this lesson are repeated below. From the Master Words, choose the appropriate word for the blank in each of the following sentences. Write the word in the numbered space provided at the right.

accessible	chafe	impinge	reverberate	staid
ascend	impetuous	pulverize	saunter	tranquil

1. Some senators think the federal government should not ...?... on the rights of states. 1. (impinge)
2. A tasty ground meal can be made from whole kernels of corn if you ...?... them. 2. (pulverize)
3. Melinda liked to ...?... about the grounds with her prize-winning French poodle. 3. (saunter)
4. The gym seemed to ...?... with cheers of thousands when the Kennedy High team appeared. 4. (reverberate)
5. The first balloon will ...?... at 2 p.m. 5. (ascend)
6. The ship idled in the ...?... seas off Madagascar. 6. (tranquil)
7. Mr. Jones' "open door" policy makes him ...?... to all. 7. (accessible)
8. Mary, always ...?..., squirted the shaving cream at the art teacher without regard to the consequences. 8. (impetuous)
9. On a cold day, the raw wind can ...?... hands and face. 9. (chafe)
10. At the ...?... white-tie-and-tails event, John's feeble jokes met with looks of disapproval. 10. (staid)

EXERCISE 6

Fill in the chart below with the Master Word that fits each set of clues. Part of speech refers to the word's usage in the lesson. Use a dictionary when necessary.

Number of Syllables	Part of Speech	Other Clues	Master Word
4	adjective	like a hasty person	1. (impetuous)
1	adjective	describes proper behavior at a funeral	2. (staid)
3	verb	do this to grain to make flour	3. (pulverize)
2	verb	elevators do this	4. (ascend)
4	adjective	what emergency exits must be	5. (accessible)
2	verb	the way window shoppers move	6. (saunter)
1	verb	ill-fitting shoes may do this	7. (chafe)
2	adjective	it is this way before a storm	8. (tranquil)
4	verb	church bells do this	9. (reverberate)
2	verb	to walk in on a private meeting, for instance	10. (impinge)

LESSON 4

Read the following selection to get the general meaning. Read it a second time, paying special attention to the words in dark type. Notice how they are used in sentences. These are Master Words. These are the words you will be working with in this lesson.

From "**The Gentleman**"
by John Henry Newman

It is almost a definition of a gentleman to say he is one who never inflicts pain. This description is both refined and, as far as it goes, accurate. He is mainly occupied in merely removing the obstacles which hinder the free and unembarrassed action of those about him, and he **concurs** with their movements rather than takes the **initiative** himself. His benefits may be considered as parallel to what are called comforts or conveniences in arrangements of a personal nature; like an easy chair or a good fire, which do their part in **dispelling** cold and fatigue, though nature provides both means of rest and animal heat without them. The true gentleman in like manner carefully avoids whatever may cause a jar or a jolt in the minds of those with whom he is cast—all clashing of opinion, or collision of feeling, all **restraint**, or suspicion, or gloom, or resentment; his great concern being to make everyone at their ease and at home. He has his eyes on all his company; he is tender toward the bashful, gentle toward the distant, and merciful toward the absurd; he can **recollect** to whom he is speaking; he guards against unreasonable **allusions**, or topics which may irritate; he is seldom prominent in conversation, and never wearisome. He makes light of favors while he does them, and seems to be receiving when he is conferring. He never speaks of himself except when **compelled**, or never defends himself by a mere **retort**; he has no ears for slander or gossip, is scrupulous in **imputing** motives to those who interfere with him, and interprets everything for the best. He is never mean or little in his disputes, never takes unfair advantage, never mistakes personalities or sharp sayings for arguments, or **insinuates** evil which he dare not say out.

EXERCISE 1

SELF-TEST: After reading the above selection, do the following. Look at the Master Words below. Underline the words that you think you know. Circle the words that you are less sure about. Draw a square around the words you don't recognize.

MASTER WORDS

allusion	**initiative**
compel	**insinuate**
concur	**recollect**
dispel	**restraint**
impute	**retort**

EXERCISE 2

Read the selection on the preceding page again, this time paying special attention to the ten Master Words. In the (a) spaces provided below, write down what you think is the meaning of the word. After you have attempted a definition for each word, look up the word in a dictionary. In the (b) spaces, copy the appropriate dictionary definition.

1. **allusion** (n.)
   a. ______
   b. indirect reference; hint; implied reference to something familiar

2. **compel** (v.)
   a. ______
   b. to force; to pressure

3. **concur** (v.)
   a. ______
   b. to coincide; to agree; to act together

4. **dispel** (v.)
   a. ______
   b. to do away with; to remove; to get rid of

5. **impute** (v.)
   a. ______
   b. to ascribe or attribute; to charge or credit

6. **initiative** (n.)
   a. ______
   b. introductory action; self-generated beginning

7. **insinuate** (v.)
   a. ______
   b. to hint indirectly; to imply

8. **recollect** (v.)
   a. ______
   b. to remember; to give consideration

9. **restraint** (n.)
   a. ______
   b. control over one's thoughts and actions; lack of freedom

10. **retort** (n.)
    a. ______
    b. a quick reply, as to an accusation; a comeback

EXERCISE 3

Use the following list of synonyms and antonyms to fill in the blanks. Some words have no antonyms. In such cases, the antonym blanks have been marked with an X.

affirm	discredit	freedom	rejoinder
agree	enterprise	hint	remember
amass	explication	imply	restriction
attribute	force	inertia	scatter
deny	forget	liberate	speechlessness

	Synonyms	Antonyms
1. **concur**	(agree)	(deny)
2. **initiative**	(enterprise)	(inertia)
3. **dispel**	(scatter)	(amass)
4. **restraint**	(restriction)	(freedom)
5. **recollect**	(remember)	(forget)
6. **allusion**	(hint)	(explication)
7. **compel**	(force)	(liberate)
8. **retort**	(rejoinder)	(speechlessness)
9. **impute**	(attribute)	(discredit) (deny)
10. **insinuate**	(imply)	(affirm)

EXERCISE 4

Decide whether the first pair in the items below are synonyms or antonyms. Then choose the Master Word that shows a similar relation to the word(s) preceding the blank.

1. pulverize	:smash	::assign	: (impute)
2. saunter	:meander	::reply	: (retort)
3. ascend	:fall	::liberty	: (restraint)
4. staid	:solemn	::suggestion	: (allusion)
5. accessible	:unreachable	::disagree	: (concur)
6. impetuous	:careful	::gather	: (dispel)
7. reverberate	:echo	::require	: (compel)
8. tranquil	:disturbed	::laziness	: (initiative)
9. impinge	:invade	::hint	: (insinuate)
10. chafe	:soothe	::overlook	: (recollect)

EXERCISE 5

The Master Words in this lesson are repeated below. From the Master Words, choose the appropriate word for the blank in each of the following sentences. Write the word in the numbered space provided at the right.

allusion	concur	impute	insinuate	restraint
compel	dispel	initiative	recollect	retort

1. The ...?... in the speech was clearly to the first chapter of Genesis. — 1. (allusion)
2. Salespeople can earn large sums, especially if they have the ...?... to work unsupervised. — 2. (initiative)
3. Although voting is a privilege and a right, no one can ...?... you to cast a vote. — 3. (compel)
4. Police officers in crowds, often baited by hoodlums, must exercise great ...?... . — 4. (restraint)
5. The town marshal wanted to ...?... the theft to a tramp. — 5. (impute)
6. His back-to-back home runs should ...?...the question about his long-ball hitting ability. — 6. (dispel)
7. All through his summary, the attorney seemed to ...?... that Holcomb, the defendant, was lying. — 7. (insinuate)
8. Do you ...?... with the minister on his color choice for the church? — 8. (concur)
9. The old gentleman was able to ...?... some delightful tales from his prairie years. — 9. (recollect)
10. A tasteless ...?... to someone is a sign of bad manners. — 10. (retort)

EXERCISE 6

To complete the crossword, choose the Master Word associated with each word or phrase below. Begin each answer in the square having the same number.

Across

2. self-starting quality
8. to bring to mind
9. hint or reference
10. to allege or charge with

Down

1. to suggest slyly
3. to remove doubt, for example
4. insist on an action
5. holding back anger requires this
6. see eye to eye
7. a sassy comeback

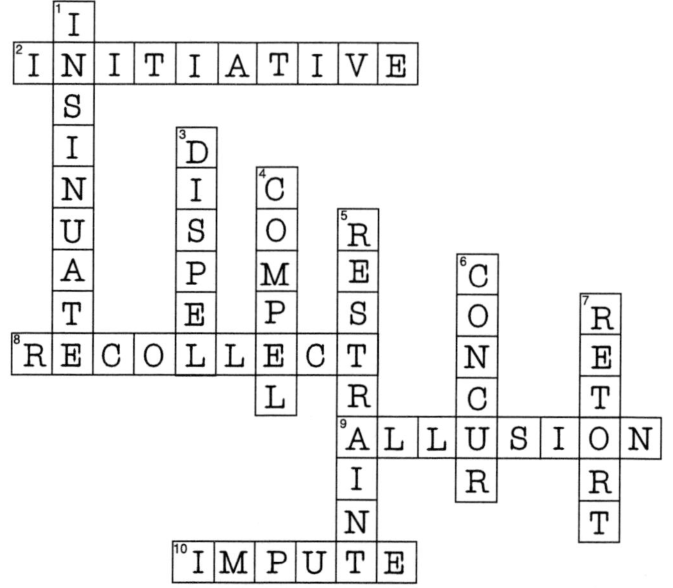

LESSON 5

Read the following selection to get the general meaning. Read it a second time, paying special attention to the words in dark type. Notice how they are used in sentences. These are Master Words. These are the words you will be working with in this section.

from ***Dear Future***
by Fred D'Aguiar

Granny came in and from her **knitted** brows he knew it was time to rest. His brother packed up the game, **proffered** that rare smile again and left. Granny tucked him in so tightly he had to strain to loosen the sheets. Then she dropped the mosquito net over his bed. To him the net was like the lid of a casket, sealed with him inside. Had the axe been one inch lower to the left or right this would have been his fate; except it would have been dark with less room to manoeuvre. He shuddered. His grandmother's tone was neither admonishing nor **sarcastic** when she watched his struggle with the sheets and asked him whether he thought he'd turned into a man. He still felt weak and any sudden move made his head throb.

He lost track of the days. Everyone was at school or in the rice fields or minding the cows or attending to the pigs or the chickens or preparing some meal in the kitchen. Everyone was everywhere but in the room with him. They were kind enough to leave him a draughts set but playing against himself only revealed the **futility** of any attempt to fool or trick his mind. They brought him a slate from school on which he practised his writing, which was better than usual without the teacher looking over his shoulder. He wrote the alphabet with a flourish as if his name **consisted** of all twenty-six letters, pretending that his chalk was really a quill and that he was signing the Declaration of Independence of his country from British rule or the **unification** of all the land's seven peoples. He also made up words by **haphazardly juxtaposing** letters plucked from his head or suggested by a portion of the wall that had caught his eye. Some mornings he'd be dreaming, something he couldn't **recount** when awake, and the smell of Granny's baked bread that filled the house at dawn would work its way into his dream, causing his mouth to water, **stirring** the desire for food and nudging him from sleep with its promise of fresh bread, melted butter and tea.

EXERCISE 1

SELF-TEST: After reading the above selection, do the following. Look at the Master Words below. Underline the words that you think you know. Circle the words that you are less sure about. Draw a square around the words you don't recognize.

MASTER WORDS	
consisted	**proffered**
futility	**recount**
haphazardly	**sarcastic**
juxtaposing	**stirring**
knitted	**unification**

EXERCISE 2

Read the selection on the preceding page again, this time paying special attention to the ten Master Words. In the (a) spaces provided below, write down what you think is the meaning of the word. After you have attempted a definition for each word, look up the word in a dictionary. In the (b) spaces, copy the appropriate dictionary definition.

1. **consisted** (v.)

   a. ______________________________

   b. composed or made up—usually used with *of*

2. **futility** (n.)

   a. ______________________________

   b. useless act or gesture

3. **haphazardly** (adv.)

   a. ______________________________

   b. in a manner marked by lack of plan, order, or direction

4. **juxtaposing** (v.)

   a. ______________________________

   b. placing side by side

5. **knitted** (adj.)

   a. ______________________________

   b. contracted into wrinkles

6. **proffered** (v.)

   a. ______________________________

   b. presented for acceptance

7. **recount** (v.)

   a. ______________________________

   b. relate in detail

8. **sarcastic** (adj.)

   a. ______________________________

   b. characterized by bitter, caustic, and often ironic language

9. **stirring** (v.)

   a. ______________________________

   b. calling up strong feelings; calling forth (as a memory)

10. **unification** (n.)

    a. ______________________________

    b. process of making into a unit or a coherent whole

EXERCISE 3

Use the following list of synonyms and antonyms to fill in the blanks. Some of the words have no antonyms. In such cases, the antonym blanks have been marked with an X.

awakening	deliberately	offered	separation	uselessness
caustic	excluded	purpose	smooth	withheld
consolidation	included	randomly	suppressing	wrinkled
convey	lining up			

	Synonyms	Antonyms
1. **knitted**	(wrinkled)	(smooth)
2. **proffered**	(offered)	(withheld)
3. **sarcastic**	(caustic)	X
4. **futility**	(uselessness)	(purpose)
5. **consisted**	(included)	(excluded)
6. **unification**	(consolidation)	(separation)
7. **haphazardly**	(randomly)	(deliberately)
8. **juxtaposing**	(lining up)	X
9. **recount**	(convey)	X
10. **stirring**	(awakening)	(suppressing)

EXERCISE 4

Decide whether the first pair in the items below are synonyms or antonyms. Then choose the Master Word that shows a similar relation to the word(s) preceding the blank.

1. dawdling	:delaying	::randomly	: (haphazardly)
2. danger	:haven	::excluded	: (consisted)
3. intentional	:deliberate	::merging	: (unification)
4. passive	:aggressive	::suppressing	: (stirring)
5. frivolous	:important	::withheld	: (proffered)
6. fractured	:broken	::wrinkled	: (knitted)
7. gesture	:movement	::convey	: (recount)
8. attentive	:distracted	::separating	: (juxtaposing)
9. righteous	:wicked	::flattering	: (sarcastic)
10. ponderous	:massive	::uselessness	: (futility)

EXERCISE 5

The Master Words in this lesson are repeated below. From the Master Words, choose the appropriate word for the blank in each of the following sentences. Write the word in the numbered space provided at the right.

consisted	haphazardly	knitted	recount	stirring
futiltiy	juxtaposition	proffered	sarcastic	unification

1. A faint scent of cinnamon reached her, ...?... up memories of visits to the bakery with her father. 1. (stirring)
2. He was depressed by the utter ...?... of his situation. 2. (futility)
3. His memory of the song ...?... of nothing more than a few words here and there. 3. (consisted)
4. By ...?... scenes of the poor and the rich families, the movie captured the Depression's effects on Americans. 4. (juxtaposing)
5. They had much to tell, but were too tired to ...?... the story. 5. (recount)
6. The child ...?... her tiny bouquet to the queen, with a charming curtsey. 6. (proffered)
7. Instead of the praise and approval she expected, she heard (a, an) ...?... edge in his voice. 7. (sarcastic)
8. His clothes were combined somewhat ...?..., as if he had dressed hurriedly in the dark. 8. (haphazardly)
9. Her face was all clenched teeth and ...?... brow, expressing intense concentration. 9. (knitted)
10. The ...?... of the newly acquired businesses under one corporate name represented the height of his career achievements. 10. (unification)

EXERCISE 6

The invented words below are formed from parts of different Master Words from this lesson. Create a definition and indicate the part of speech for each word. The first one is done for you.

stircastic *(adj.) arousing scornful feelings*

futilification (n.) the bringing together of useless elements

juxtacount (v.) to tell two stories interwoven together

sarcazardly (adv.) carelessly scornful

Now invent your own words by combining parts of the Master Words. Create a definition for each, and indicate the word's part of speech. You may use any of the word parts above in new combinations.

Answers will vary.

LESSON 6

Read the following selection to get the general meaning. Read it a second time, paying special attention to the words in dark type. Notice how they are used in sentences. These are Master Words. These are the words you will be working with in this section.

from ***Nelson Mandela: "No Easy Walk to Freedom"***
by Barry Denenberg

In 1941, when Mandela was twenty-three, Johannesburg was well on its way to becoming one of the world's most modern cities. Africans called it "Egoli" — City of Gold. Sixty years earlier gold had been discovered, and the city had grown rapidly. Hundreds of thousands of Africans from the surrounding rural areas **migrated** to Johannesburg, hoping to find work in the factories and the mines.

Mandela took a job as a guard outside one of the **compounds** where the black miners were housed. Armed with a whistle and a **knobbed** stick, he was there to make sure everyone behaved themselves. The living conditions shocked him. Miners were not allowed to have their families with them. Food and shelter were provided, but not much else. If you quit you risked being sent to jail. There were no sick days, vacations, or **pensions**. The men slept sometimes fifty to a room, on double-decker concrete bunks, and hid their belongings at night so they wouldn't be robbed.

Blacks who didn't work in the mines didn't fare much better. By day, blacks and whites crowded into bustling downtown Johannesburg. But nighttime told a different story. As darkness fell whites retreated to the safety and comfort of the suburbs. Blacks returned to their townships.

Townships are areas near a city—**sprawling** slums with row upon row of tiny, boxlike houses. Families often sleep three and four to a room, sometimes more. There is usually no running water, electricity, or **sanitary facilities**. Disease, crime, the police, and poverty are the constant companions of the people in the townships.

When Mandela arrived, the City of Gold was experiencing a **surge** in population. Many who came were not only seeking work in the mines. Many, like Mandela, were educated, **ambitious**, and becoming more politically aware every day. They were frustrated by the world of **legalized** racism with which they were being forced to **cope**.

EXERCISE 1

SELF-TEST: After reading the above selection, do the following. Look at the Master Words below. Underline the words that you think you know. Circle the words that you are less sure about. Draw a square around the words you don't recognize.

MASTER WORDS	
ambitious	**migrated**
compounds	**pensions**
cope	**sanitary facilities**
knobbed	**sprawling**
legalized	**surge**

EXERCISE 2

Read the selection on the preceding page again, this time paying special attention to the ten Master Words. In the (a) spaces provided below, write down what you think is the meaning of the word. After you have attempted a definition for each word, look up the word in a dictionary. In the (b) spaces, copy the appropriate dictionary definition.

1. **ambitious** (adj.)

   a. ______

   b. eager to succeed

2. **compounds** (n.)

   a. ______

   b. fenced groups of buildings

3. **cope** (v.)

   a. ______

   b. maintain; deal with; attempt to overcome

4. **knobbed** (adj.)

   a. ______

   b. bumpy

5. **legalized** (adj.)

   a. ______

   b. acceptable according to law

6. **migrated** (v.)

   a. ______

   b. moved from place to place

7. **pensions** (n.)

   a. ______

   b. retirement payments

8. **sanitary facilities** (n.)

   a. ______

   b. toilets

9. **sprawling** (adj.)

   a. ______

   b. carelessly spread out

10. **surge** (n.)

    a. ______

    b. a wavelike swell or sudden increase

EXERCISE 3

Use the following list of synonyms and antonyms to fill in the blanks. Some of the words have no antonyms. In such cases, the antonym blanks have been marked with an X.

aimless	compact	increase	moved	smooth
aspiring	decline	lawful	payments	spreading
bumpy	illegal	maintain	remained	toilets
camps				

	Synonyms	Antonyms
1. **migrated**	(moved)	(remained)
2. **compounds**	(camps)	X
3. **knobbed**	(bumpy)	(smooth)
4. **pensions**	(payments)	X
5. **sprawling**	(spreading)	(compact)
6. **sanitary facilities**	(toilets)	X
7. **surge**	(increase)	(decline)
8. **ambitious**	(aspiring)	(aimless)
9. **legalized**	(lawful)	(illegal)
10. **cope**	(maintain)	X

EXERCISE 4

Decide whether the first pair in the items below are synonyms or antonyms. Then choose the Master Word that shows a similar relation to the word(s) preceding the blank.

1. dubious	:doubtful	::increase	: (surge)
2. paradox	:contradiction	::payments	: (pensions)
3. notorious	:beloved	::remained	: (migrated)
4. unbeatable	:invincible	::spreading	: (sprawling)
5. respect	:homage	::groups of buildings	: (compounds)
6. hindrance	:obstacle	::maintain	: (cope)
7. wary	:trusting	::aimless	: (ambitious)
8. signal	:cue	::toilets	: (sanitary facilities)
9. attributes	:qualities	::bumpy	: (knobbed)
10. gather	:disperse	::illegal	: (legalized)

EXERCISE 5

The Master Words in this lesson are repeated below. From the Master Words, choose the appropriate word for the blank in each of the following sentences. Write the word in the numbered space provided at the right.

ambitious	cope	legalized	pensions	sprawling
compounds	knobbed	migrated	sanitary facilities	surge

1. The cabin was without phones, electricity, and running water, but without ...?..., life there was just too primitive. 1. (sanitary facilities)
2. The family of geese landed on the familiar pond, where they stopped every year as they ...?... south for the winter. 2. (migrated)
3. She didn't know how she would ...?... without an ice cream store within walking distance. 3. (cope)
4. He was just what the company was looking for—bright, ...?..., and willing to work long hours. 4. (ambitious)
5. The garden was beyond reclaiming, with squash plants and strawberry runners ...?... everywhere. 5. (sprawling)
6. Her hands were ...?... and wrinkled, showing the ravages of age and illness. 6. (knobbed)
7. The 21st Amendment once again ...?... the sale and manufacture of liquor. 7. (legalized)
8. They felt a great ...?... of pride as they watched their daughter win the race. 8. (surge)
9. The prison was divided into several walled ...?..., each housing one hundred prisoners. 9. (compounds)
10. While teachers' salaries were low, their ...?... were among the best in the city. 10. (pensions)

EXERCISE 6

Fill in the chart below with the Master Word that fits each set of clues. Part of speech refers to the way the word is used in this lesson. Use a dictionary when necessary.

Number of Syllables	Part of Speech	Other Clues	Master Word
2	Noun	What workers need when they retire	1. (pensions)
3	Adjective	What someone might need to be to succeed in business	2. (ambitious)
3	Adjective	What gambling has become in many states	3. (legalized)
1	Verb	What some people can't do when they face tough times	4. (cope)
2	Adjective	What cities seem to be doing	5. (sprawling)
2	Noun	What a prison might be divided into	6. (compounds)
3	Verb	What animals have done to seek food and shelter	7. (migrated)
1	Noun	What happens when things increase very fast	8. (surge)

LESSON 7

Read the following selection to get the general meaning. Read it a second time, paying special attention to the words in dark type. Notice how they are used in sentences. These are Master Words. These are the words you will be working with in this lesson.

From "**A Mystery of Heroism**"
by Stephen Crane

The leading company of the infantry regiment was somewhat exposed, and the colonel ordered it moved more fully under the shelter of the hill. There was the clank of steel against steel.

A lieutenant of the battery rode down and passed them, holding his right arm carefully in his left hand. And it was as if this arm was not at all a part of him, but belonged to another man. His sober and reflective charger went slowly. The officer's face was **grimy** and perspiring, and his uniform was **tousled** as if he had been in direct grapple with an enemy. He smiled **grimly** when the men stared at him. He turned his horse toward the meadow.

Collins, of A Company, said: "I wisht I had a drink. I bet there's water in that there ol' well yonder!"

"Yes; but how you goin' to git it?"

For the little meadow which **intervened** was now suffering a terrible **onslaught** of shells. Its green and beautiful calm had vanished **utterly**. Brown earth was being flung in monstrous handfuls. And there was a **massacre** of the young blades of grass. They were being torn, burned, **obliterated**. Some **curious** fortune of the battle had made this gentle little meadow the object of the red hate of the shells, and each one as it exploded seemed like an **imprecation** in the face of a maiden.

The wounded officer who was riding across this expanse said to himself: "Why, they couldn't shoot any harder if the whole army was massed here!"

EXERCISE 1

SELF-TEST: After reading the above selection, do the following. Look at the Master Words below. Underline the words that you think you know. Circle the words that you are less sure about. Draw a square around the words you don't recognize.

MASTER WORDS

curious	**massacre**
grim	**obliterate**
grimy	**onslaught**
imprecation	**tousled**
intervene	**utterly**

EXERCISE 2

Read the selection on the preceding page again, this time paying special attention to the ten Master Words. In the (a) spaces provided below, write down what you think is the meaning of the word. After you have attempted a definition for each word, look up the word in a dictionary. In the (b) spaces, copy the appropriate dictionary definition.

1. **curious** (adj.)

   a. ________________

   b. strange; rare; unusual

2. **grim** (adj.)

   a. ________________

   b. unyielding; stern; harsh and forbidding; fierce

3. **grimy** (adj.)

   a. ________________

   b. deeply soiled; dirty

4. **imprecation** (n.)

   a. ________________

   b. a curse or oath

5. **intervene** (v.)

   a. ________________

   b. to come between; to occur between points

6. **massacre** (n.)

   a. ________________

   b. collective slaughter, usually of human beings

7. **obliterate** (v.)

   a. ________________

   b. to cancel, erase, or wipe out

8. **onslaught** (n.)

   a. ________________

   b. a furious attack

9. **tousled** (adj.)

   a. ________________

   b. disheveled; rumpled

10. **utterly** (adv.)

    a. ________________

    b. totally; fully; completely

EXERCISE 3

Use the following list of synonyms and antonyms to fill in the blanks. Some words have no antonyms. In such cases, the antonym blanks have been marked with an X.

assault	expunge	praise	slaughter
bizarre	interpose	protection	spotless
curse	merry	refrain	stern
defense	neat	restore	totally
dirty	partially	rumpled	usual

	Synonyms	Antonyms
1. **grimy**	(dirty)	(spotless)
2. **tousled**	(rumpled)	(neat)
3. **grim**	(stern)	(merry)
4. **intervene**	(interpose)	(refrain)
5. **onslaught**	(assault)	(defense)
6. **utterly**	(totally)	(partially)
7. **massacre**	(slaughter)	(protection)
8. **obliterate**	(expunge)	(restore)
9. **curious**	(bizarre)	(usual)
10. **imprecation**	(curse)	(praise)

EXERCISE 4

Decide whether the first pair in the items below are synonyms or antonyms. Then choose the Master Word that shows a similar relation to the word(s) preceding the blank.

1. perceive	:understand	::come between	: (intervene)
2. brood	:think over	::oath	: (imprecation)
3. vent	:restrain	::halfway	: (utterly)
4. agitation	:peacefulness	::ordinary	: (curious)
5. pretext	:justification	::mass murder	: (massacre)
6. impertinent	:respectful	::mild	: (grim)
7. reprimand	:compliment	::orderly	: (tousled)
8. utter	:say	::attack	: (onslaught)
9. spleen	:irritation	::erase	: (obliterate)
10. linger	:hurry	::clean	: (grimy)

EXERCISE 5

The Master Words in this lesson are repeated below. From the Master Words, choose the appropriate word for the blank in each of the following sentences. Write the word in the numbered space provided at the right.

curious	grimy	intervene	obliterate	tousled
grim	imprecation	massacre	onslaught	utterly

1. The commercial prompted "new whiteness" for even the most ...?... clothes. — 1. (grimy)
2. Someone in the angry crowd hurled an unmentionable ...?... at the policeman. — 2. (imprecation)
3. After riding in the crowded bus for thirty miles in our band uniforms, we appeared ...?... and frumpy in the parade. — 3. (tousled)
4. Webster High's young team was buried under a first quarter ...?... of Dowling touchdowns. — 4. (onslaught)
5. Death is often portrayed as "the ...?... reaper," a skeleton wrapped in a sheet and wielding a scythe. — 5. (grim)
6. A teacher should not ...?... in a matter between a student and another teacher—unless asked. — 6. (intervene)
7. Holmes wanted to examine the ...?... circumstance surrounding the disappearance of the diamond. — 7. (curious)
8. The ...?... of Native Americans at Sand Creek was a blight on U.S. history. — 8. (massacre)
9. The new freeway will take many homes in its path and ...?... a whole neighborhood. — 9. (obliterate)
10. The corn crop was ...?... ruined by drought, insects, heat, and weeds. — 10. (utterly)

EXERCISE 6

To complete the word spiral, choose the Master Word associated with each phrase below. Start with 1 and fill in each answer clockwise. Be careful! Each new word may overlap the previous word by one or more letters.

1. kids' hands, sometimes
2. to the limit
3. mediators do this
4. like a determined look
5. angry words
6. attack at Pearl Harbor, for instance
7. your hair in the morning
8. a bit odd
9. Wounded Knee was one
10. atomic bombs and plagues do this

1. G	R	I	M	Y	2. U	T	T	E
A	T	I	6. O	N	S	L	A	R
C	O	U	S	9. M	A	S	U	L
E	I	I	T	E	R	S	G	Y
R	R	L	E	T	A	A	H	3. I
P	U	B	10. O	E	R	C	7. T	N
M	8. C	D	E	L	S	U	O	T
5. I	R	4. G	E	N	E	V	R	E

LESSON 8

Read the following selection to get the general meaning. Read it a second time, paying special attention to the words in dark type. Notice how they are used in sentences. These are Master Words. These are the words you will be working with in this lesson.

From **The Deerslayer**
by James Fenimore Cooper

The young men showed an impatience to begin to torture, that Rivenoak understood; and as his elder associates manifested no disposition to permit any longer delay, he was compelled to give the signal for the infernal work to proceed.

It was one of the common **expedients** of the savages, on such occasions, to put the nerves of their victims to the severest proofs. On the other hand, it was a matter of Indian pride to betray no yielding to terror or pain, but for the prisoner to provoke his enemies to such acts of violence as would soonest produce death. Many a warrior had been known to bring his own sufferings to a more speedy **termination**, by **taunting reproaches** and **reviling** language, when he found that his physical system was giving way under the agony of sufferings produced by a hellish **ingenuity** that might well **eclipse** all that has been said of the **infernal** devices of religious **persecution**. This happy expedient of taking refuge from the **ferocity** of his foes in their passions was denied Deerslayer, however, by his peculiar notions of the duty of a white man; and he had stoutly made up his mind to endure everything, in preference to disgracing his color.

No sooner did the young men understand that they were at liberty to commence, than some of the boldest and most forward among them sprang into the arena, tomahawk in hand. Here they prepared to throw that dangerous weapon, the object being to strike the tree as near as possible to the victim's head, without absolutely hitting him. . . .

EXERCISE 1

SELF-TEST: After reading the above selection, do the following. Look at the Master Words below. Underline the words that you think you know. Circle the words that you are less sure about. Draw a square around the words you don't recognize.

MASTER WORDS

eclipse	**persecution**
expedient	**reproach**
ferocity	**revile**
infernal	**taunt**
ingenuity	**termination**

EXERCISE 2

Read the selection on the preceding page again, this time paying special attention to the ten Master Words. In the (a) spaces provided below, write down what you think is the meaning of the word. After you have attempted a definition for each word, look up the word in a dictionary. In the (b) spaces, copy the appropriate dictionary definition.

1. **eclipse** (v.)
   a. ____________________
   b. to surpass; to overshadow; to excel
2. **expedient** (n.)
   a. ____________________
   b. a means to an end; that which is advantageous
3. **ferocity** (n.)
   a. ____________________
   b. savageness; wildness
4. **infernal** (adj.)
   a. ____________________
   b. devilish; like a fiend; also, pesky or detestable
5. **ingenuity** (n.)
   a. ____________________
   b. inventiveness; cleverness
6. **persecution** (n.)
   a. ____________________
   b. harassment; oppression; ill-treatment
7. **reproach** (n.)
   a. ____________________
   b. reprimand; blame
8. **revile** (v.)
   a. ____________________
   b. to speak against or scold
9. **taunt** (v.)
   a. ____________________
   b. to make fun of; to sneer; to jeer at
10. **termination** (n.)
    a. ____________________
    b. limit; end; final phase

EXERCISE 3

Use the following list of synonyms and antonyms to fill in the blanks. Some words have no antonyms. In such cases, the antonym blanks have been marked with an X.

approve	end	lag	savagery
beginning	heavenly	method	surpass
berate	incompetence	oppression	timidity
cheer	inventiveness	praise	tolerance
diabolical	jeer	rebuke	

	Synonyms	Antonyms
1. **expedient**	(method)	X
2. **termination**	(end)	(beginning)
3. **taunt**	(jeer)	(cheer) (approve) (praise)
4. **reproach**	(rebuke)	(praise)
5. **revile**	(berate) (rebuke)	(approve) (praise)
6. **ingenuity**	(inventiveness)	(incompetence)
7. **eclipse**	(surpass)	(lag)
8. **infernal**	(diabolical)	(heavenly)
9. **persecution**	(oppression)	(tolerance)
10. **ferocity**	(savagery)	(timidity)

EXERCISE 4

Decide whether the first pair in the items below are synonyms or antonyms. Then choose the Master Word that shows a similar relation to the word(s) preceding the blank.

1. grim	:gentle	::approval	: (reproach)
2. utterly	:partly	::start	: (termination)
3. intervene	:break into	::fierceness	: (ferocity)
4. onslaught	:invasion	::cruelty	: (persecution)
5. imprecation	:curse	::means	: (expedient)
6. massacre	:annihilation	::outdo	: (eclipse)
7. tousled	:tidy	::encourage	: (taunt)
8. grimy	:unsoiled	::bless	: (revile)
9. obliterate	:wipe out	::fiendish	: (infernal)
10. curious	:normal	::unimaginativeness	: (ingenuity)

EXERCISE 5

The Master Words in this lesson are repeated below. From the Master Words, choose the appropriate word for the blank in each of the following sentences. Write the word in the numbered space provided at the right.

eclipse	ferocity	ingenuity	reproach	taunt
expedient	infernal	persecution	revile	termination

1. Yankee ...?... permitted GIs on islands to make washing machines from windmills. 1. (ingenuity)
2. The ...?... of his contract is slated for January 1 of next year. 2. (termination)
3. Few Christians escaped ...?... by the Romans. 3. (persecution)
4. He received a mild ...?... for forgetting to bring his homework. 4. (reproach)
5. The ...?... of the Australian fighting man is a marvel of modern warfare. 5. (ferocity)
6. Mann's excellent time in the hundred-yard dash is certain to ...?... the school record. 6. (eclipse)
7. Personal decisions—as well as government decisions—are frequently based on (a, an) ...?... rather than on what is right. 7. (expedient)
8. Dante's great work is of a journey through hell in the ...?... regions of the earth. 8. (infernal)
9. It usually does little good to ...?... students for minor wrongs, except as an excuse for teachers to sharpen their tongues. 9. (revile)
10. His practice was to ...?... little girls by tugging on their hair. 10. (taunt)

EXERCISE 6

Write the Master Word that is associated with each word group below. Then list three things that might be associated with the review word that follows.

1. inventing, decoding, detecting (ingenuity)
2. finale, death, fired (termination)
3. solution, plea bargain, means to an end (expedient)
4. blame, lecture, scold (reproach) (revile)
5. Hitler, Satan, demon (infernal)
6. record, all-time best, top of the charts (eclipse)
7. condemn, scorn, spit upon (revile) (reproach)
8. nerd, egghead, bully (taunt)
9. tornado, lion, warrior (ferocity)
10. Pilgrims, Jews, minorities (persecution)

Review word: obliterate (Lesson 7)

(bomb) (hurricane) (time)

(Note: Answers may vary.)

LESSON 9

Read the following selection to get the general meaning. Read it a second time, paying special attention to the words in dark type. Notice how they are used in sentences. These are Master Words. These are the words you will be working with in this section.

from ***Falling Leaves: The True Story of an Unwanted Chinese Daughter***
by Adeline Yen Mah

On each of the five days we spent in Shanghai I collected my aunt and she would take her hot bath in our hotel room. There wasn't time enough for all we wanted to say to each other.

I offered to buy my aunt an apartment in Shanghai which was being **erected** at a **site** close to our hotel. She declined, saying that she had no wish to leave her neighbourhood. "I have lived in the same lane since 1943," she told me. "This is my home. The only place I wish to move to is our old house at No. 15. If you can get it back for me, I shall die happy." Two years later, Bob and I were able to **procure** the house on her **behalf** and she lived there till she died.

I asked her if she regretted staying behind in Shanghai.

Her answer was an unequivocal *no.* "It has been bad here. All those **campaigns** and struggle meetings. The **savagery** of the Cultural Revolution. Poverty, hardship and fear. Quite honestly though, all the miseries put together were more **tolerable** than living under the same roof as your Niang. I am content with *cu cha dan fan* (coarse tea and plain rice).

"I often think of life as a **deposit** of time. We are each **allocated** so many years, just like a fixed sum in a bank. When twenty-four hours have passed I have spent one more day. I read in the *People's Daily* that the average life **expectancy** for a Chinese woman is seventy-two. I am already seventy-four years old. I spent all my deposits two years ago and am on bonus time. Every day is already a gift. What is there to complain of?"

EXERCISE 1

SELF-TEST: After reading the above selection, do the following. Look at the Master Words below. Underline the words that you think you know. Circle the words that you are less sure about. Draw a square around the words you don't recognize.

MASTER WORDS

allocated	**expectancy**
behalf	**procure**
campaigns	**savagery**
deposit	**site**
erected	**tolerable**

EXERCISE 2

Read the selection on the preceding page again, this time paying special attention to the ten Master Words. In the (a) spaces provided below, write down what you think is the meaning of the word. After you have attempted a definition for each word, look up the word in a dictionary. In the (b) spaces, copy the appropriate dictionary definition.

1. **allocated** (v.)
   a. ______
   b. measured out; distributed
2. **behalf** (n.)
   a. ______
   b. benefit; interest
3. **campaigns** (n.)
   a. ______
   b. organized efforts to bring about a particular result
4. **deposit** (n.)
   a. ______
   b. something set aside for safekeeping
5. **erected** (v.)
   a. ______
   b. built
6. **expectancy** (n.)
   a. ______
   b. anticipated measure or amount
7. **procure** (v.)
   a. ______
   b. get possession of; acquire
8. **savagery** (n.)
   a. ______
   b. cruelty; brutality
9. **site** (n.)
   a. ______
   b. the planned location of something
10. **tolerable** (adj.)
    a. ______
    b. capable of being endured

EXERCISE 3

Use the following list of synonyms and antonyms to fill in the blanks. Some of the words have no antonyms. In such cases, the antonym blanks have been marked with an X.

acquire	built	detriment	gentleness	measured	unbearable
benefit	denied	efforts	location	savings	withdrawal
brutality	destroyed	endurable	lose		

	Synonyms	Antonyms
1. **erected**	(built)	(destroyed)
2. **site**	(location)	X
3. **procure**	(acquire)	(lose)
4. **behalf**	(benefit)	(detriment)
5. **campaigns**	(efforts)	X
6. **savagery**	(brutality)	(gentleness)
7. **tolerable**	(endurable)	(unbearable)
8. **deposit**	(savings)	(withdrawal)
9. **allocated**	(measured)	(denied)
10. **expectancy**	(probability)	X

EXERCISE 4

Decide whether the first pair in the items below are synonyms or antonyms. Then choose the Master Word that shows a similar relation to the word(s) preceding the blank.

1. beneficial	:toxic	::kindness	: (savagery)
2. privileged	:elite	::movements	: (campaigns)
3. facilitate	:impede	::unendurable	: (tolerable)
4. loathe	:despise	::benefit	: (behalf)
5. coveted	:envied	::savings	: (deposit)
6. cautious	:negligent	::lose	: (procure)
7. expended	:used up	::designated	: (allocated)
8. risky	:precarious	::whereabouts	: (site)
9. rubbish	:debris	::probability	: (expectancy)
10. polluted	:pristine	::dismantled	: (erected)

EXERCISE 5

The Master Words in this lesson are repeated below. From the Master Words, choose the appropriate word for the blank in each of the following sentences. Write the word in the numbered space provided at the right.

allocated	campaigns	erected	procure	site
behalf	deposit	expectancy	savagery	tolerable

1. The results of the school election were awaited with great ...?... . 1. (expectancy)
2. The inheritance check made for a nice ...?... in his bank account. 2. (deposit)
3. They all had to put on hard hats when they approached the building ...?... . 3. (site)
4. She tended to think of nature as gentle and idyllic, but watching the ...?... of the lion killing and eating its prey was shocking. 4. (savagery)
5. The monument was ...?... on the town square, at the site of the historic speech. 5. (erected)
6. Since the school's budget was small, paper and other supplies had to be ...?... for each classroom. 6. (allocated)
7. The combination of heat and humidity made the climate barely ...?... . 7. (tolerable)
8. His studio managed to ...?... the rights to the story, even though every other studio in the city was bidding for them. 8. (procure)
9. The host accepted the award on ...?... of the artist, who was on tour in Japan. 9. (behalf)
10. The election ...?... seemed to get more elaborate and competitive each year. 10. (campaigns)

EXERCISE 6

To complete this puzzle, fill in the Master Word associated with each phrase or sentence. Then unscramble the circled letters to form another Master Word from this lesson.

1. Another way of saying "for the benefit of" is "on b e h a (l) f of."
2. Built-up is the same as e r e c t e (d) .
3. Before going on the field trip, you must p r (o) c u r e your parents' permission.
4. Another word for cruelty: s a v (a) g e r y .
5. You can make a d (e) p o s i t into a checking or savings account.
6. Sitting in class on a really hot day feels barely t o (l) e r a b l e .
7. When you grow quickly, you might say your clothes have a short life e x p e c t (a) n c y .
8. A sign might read, "Building s i (t) e : Proceed with caution."
9. (C) a m p a i g n s are launched when people want to accomplish serious goals.

Now unscramble the scrambled Master Word and write it here: (allocated)

LESSON 10

Read the following selection to get the general meaning. Read it a second time, paying special attention to the words in dark type. Notice how they are used in sentences. These are Master Words. These are the words you will be working with in this lesson.

From **The Declaration of Independence**
by Thomas Jefferson

When, in the **Course** of human events, it becomes necessary for one people to **dissolve** the political bands which have connected them with another, and to assume among the Powers of the earth, the separate and equal station to which the Laws of Nature and of Nature's God **entitle** them, a decent respect to the opinions of mankind requires that they should declare the causes which **impel** them to the separation.

We hold these truths to be self-evident, that all men are created equal, that they are **endowed** by their Creator with certain **inalienable** Rights, that among these are Life, Liberty and the pursuit of Happiness. That to **secure** these Rights, Governments are **instituted** among Men, **deriving** their just powers from the consent of the governed, That whenever any Form of Government becomes destructive of these ends, it is the Right of the People to **alter** or abolish it, and to institute new Government, laying its foundation on such principles and organizing its powers in such form, as to them shall seem most likely to effect their Safety and Happiness.

EXERCISE 1

SELF-TEST: After reading the above selection, do the following. Look at the Master Words below. Underline the words that you think you know. Circle the words that you are less sure about. Draw a square around the words you don't recognize.

MASTER WORDS

alter	**entitle**
course	**impel**
derive	**inalienable**
dissolve	**institute**
endow	**secure**

EXERCISE 2

Read the selection on the preceding page again, this time paying special attention to the ten Master Words. In the (a) spaces provided below, write down what you think is the meaning of the word. After you have attempted a definition for each word, look up the word in a dictionary. In the (b) spaces, copy the appropriate dictionary definition.

1. **alter** (v.)

   a. ______

   b. to make different; to modify; to change without loss of identity

2. **course** (n.)

   a. ______

   b. direction or movement, as from A to B

3. **derive** (v.)

   a. ______

   b. to come from a source; to trace the origin of

4. **dissolve** (v.)

   a. ______

   b. to break into parts; to disappear or vanish

5. **endow** (v.)

   a. ______

   b. to give to; to provide with

6. **entitle** (v.)

   a. ______

   b. to give a right to; to provide with a title or claim

7. **impel** (v.)

   a. ______

   b. to force; to cause to move; to drive

8. **inalienable** (adj.)

   a. ______

   b. not to be taken away or parted from

9. **institute** (v.)

   a. ______

   b. to set up; to found; to begin; to initiate

10. **secure** (v.)

    a. ______

    b. to acquire or obtain

EXERCISE 3

Use the following list of synonyms and antonyms to fill in the blanks. Some words have no antonyms. In such cases, the antonym blanks have been marked with an X.

acquire	direction	fix	revocable
begin	discourage	guaranteed	surrender
bestow	disperse	merge	urge
cancel	disqualify	qualify	vary
chartlessness	draw	return	withhold

	Synonyms	Antonyms
1. **course**	(direction)	(chartlessness)
2. **dissolve**	(disperse)	(merge)
3. **entitle**	(qualify)	(disqualify)
4. **impel**	(urge)	(discourage)
5. **endow**	(bestow)	(withhold)
6. **inalienable**	(guaranteed)	(revocable)
7. **secure**	(acquire)	(surrender)
8. **institute**	(begin)	(cancel)
9. **derive**	(draw)	(return)
10. **alter**	(vary)	(fix)

EXERCISE 4

Decide whether the first pair in the items below are synonyms or antonyms. Then choose the Master Word that shows a similar relation to the word(s) preceding the blank.

1. hoard	:shortage	::terminate	: (institute) (derive)
2. stalk	:march	::permit	: (entitle)
3. pry	:spy	::give	: (endow)
4. tantalize	:torment	::modify	: (alter)
5. conspire	:scheme	::route	: (course)
6. miser	:squanderer	::restrain	: (impel)
7. balk	:hasten	::form	: (dissolve)
8. prevalent	:infrequent	::conclude	: (derive) (institute)
9. termagant	:shrew	::permanent	: (inalienable)
10. meager	:plentiful	::give up	: (secure)

EXERCISE 5

The Master Words in this lesson are repeated below. From the Master Words, choose the appropriate word for the blank in each of the following sentences. Write the word in the numbered space provided at the right.

alter	derive	endow	impel	institute
course	dissolve	entitle	inalienable	secure

1. The ...?... of history has frequently turned on small events that seemed unimportant at the time. 1. (course)
2. If the bill is not paid soon, he promises to ...?... court proceedings. 2. (institute)
3. If you keep your eyes open, you can ...?... some good bargains just after Christmas. 3. (secure)
4. During periods of unemployment, a family may have to ...?... its budget to remain out of debt. 4. (alter)
5. This coupon ...?...(s) you to a free dinner at Michael's Restaurant. 5. (entitle)
6. Wealthy people sometimes ...?... their favorite universities with large sums of cash. 6. (endow)
7. Before the election could be held, it was necessary to ...?... the parliament. 7. (dissolve)
8. Through a complex process, we can ...?... sugar from beets. 8. (derive)
9. "Presumed innocence" is (a,an) ...?... protection provided by the courts. 9. (inalienable)
10. Dishonesty in office may ...?... you to change your political loyalty. 10. (impel)

EXERCISE 6

Order the words in each item from *least* to *most.* Use the abbreviations *L* for "least" and *M* for "most." Leave the line before the word of the middle degree blank. The first word provides a clue about how to arrange the words. See the example.

relaxed: ____firm L taut M loose
(*Taut* indicates the least relaxed; *loose* indicates the most relaxed.)

1. direct:	____ramble	(L) maze	(M) course
2. stable:	(L) dissolve	(M) solidify	____soften
3. change:	____alter	(L) preserve	(M) transform
4. original:	(M) create	(L) copy	____derive
5. protected:	(L) tolerated	(M) inalienable	____granted
6. generous:	(L) rob	(M) endow	____withhold
7. approval:	(M) entitle	(L) disbar	____consent
8. definite:	(M) institute	(L) imagine	____propose
9. solid:	(L) desire	(M) secure	____promise
10. demanding:	____require	(M) impel	(L) suggest

(Note: In some cases, answers may vary.)

LESSON 11

Read the following selection to get the general meaning. Read it a second time, paying special attention to the words in dark type. Notice how they are used in sentences. These are Master Words. These are the words you will be working with in this lesson.

From **The Return of the Native**
by Thomas Hardy

A Saturday afternoon in November was approaching the time of twilight, and the **vast tract** of unenclosed wild known as Egdon Heath embrowned itself moment by moment. Overhead the hollow stretch of whitish cloud shutting out the sky was as a tent which had the whole **heath** for its floor.

The heaven being spread with this **pallid** screen and the earth with the darkest vegetation, their meeting-line at the horizon was clearly marked. In such contrast the heath wore the appearance of an instalment of night which had taken up its place before its astronomical hour was come: darkness had to a great extent arrived hereon, while day stood distinct in the sky. . . . The distant rims of the world and of the **firmament** seemed to be a division in time no less than a division in matter. The face of the heath by its mere complexion added half an hour to evening; it could in like manner **retard** the dawn, sadden noon, anticipate the frowning of storms scarcely **generated**, and intensify the **opacity** of a moonless midnight to a cause of shaking and dread.

In fact, **precisely** at this **transitional** point of its nightly roll into darkness the great and particular glory of the Egdon waste began, and nobody could be said to understand the heath who had not been there at such a time.

EXERCISE 1

SELF-TEST: After reading the above selection, do the following. Look at the Master Words below. Underline the words that you think you know. Circle the words that you are less sure about. Draw a square around the words you don't recognize.

MASTER WORDS

firmament	**precise**
generate	**retard**
heath	**tract**
opacity	**transitional**
pallid	**vast**

EXERCISE 2

Read the selection on the preceding page again, this time paying special attention to the ten Master Words. In the (a) spaces provided below, write down what you think is the meaning of the word. After you have attempted a definition for each word, look up the word in a dictionary. In the (b) spaces, copy the appropriate dictionary definition.

1. **firmament** (n.)

   a. __________

   b. the sky or heavens

2. **generate** (v.)

   a. __________

   b. to produce or originate; to manufacture

3. **heath** (n.)

   a. __________

   b. a tract of open wasteland

4. **opacity** (n.)

   a. __________

   b. state of not letting light through; impenetrability

5. **pallid** (adj.)

   a. __________

   b. lacking color; pale

6. **precise** (adj.)

   a. __________

   b. exact; clear; well-defined

7. **retard** (v.)

   a. __________

   b. to slow down; to decelerate

8. **tract** (n.)

   a. __________

   b. land; region or area without definite boundaries

9. **transitional** (adj.)

   a. __________

   b. related to change

10. **vast** (adj.)

    a. __________

    b. large; huge in bulk; unbounded; immense

EXERCISE 3

Use the following list of synonyms and antonyms to fill in the blanks. Some words have no antonyms. In such cases, the antonym blanks have been marked with an X.

accelerate	disconnected	immense	originate
careful	earth	inexact	rosy
delay	expanse	linking	sallow
destroy	garden	molehill	small
dimness	heaven	moor	transparency

	Synonyms	Antonyms
1. **vast**	(immense)	(small)
2. **tract**	(expanse)	(molehill)
3. **heath**	(moor)	(garden)
4. **pallid**	(sallow)	(rosy)
5. **firmament**	(heaven)	(earth)
6. **retard**	(delay)	(accelerate)
7. **generate**	(originate)	(destroy)
8. **opacity**	(dimness)	(transparency)
9. **precise**	(careful)	(inexact)
10. **transitional**	(linking)	(disconnected)

EXERCISE 4

Decide whether the first pair in the items below are synonyms or antonyms. Then choose the Master Word that shows a similar relation to the word(s) preceding the blank.

1. dissolve	:consolidate	::speed	: (retard)
2. course	:path	::pale	: (pallid)
3. derive	:originate	::connecting	: (transitional)
4. endow	:award	::area	: (tract)
5. entitle	:authorize	::sky	: (firmament)
6. alter	:maintain	::tiny	: (vast)
7. institute	:establish	::grassland	: (heath)
8. secure	:lose	::clearness	: (opacity)
9. impel	:force	::actual	: (precise)
10. inalienable	:retractable	::wipe out	: (generate)

EXERCISE 5

The Master Words in this lesson are repeated below. From the Master Words, choose the appropriate word for the blank in each of the following sentences. Write the word in the numbered space provided at the right.

firmament	heath	pallid	retard	transitional
generate	opacity	precise	tract	vast

1. The Apollo missions have helped explain many questions about the ...?... . 1. (firmament)
2. Much land in north England is still open ...?..., used only for grazing or as a tourist attraction. 2. (heath)
3. On the first warm, sunny day in May, his ...?... skin turned fiery red from too much sun. 3. (pallid)
4. A small ...?... of land was set aside to be used for future oil development. 4. (tract)
5. A good composition should have ...?... devices to provide smoothness. 5. (transitional)
6. Television was once referred to by an important executive as (a, an) "...?... wasteland." 6. (vast)
7. Good advertising is certain to ...?... a large amount of business. 7. (generate)
8. Material of high ...?... should be used for window shades. 8. (opacity)
9. Speech must be ...?... in order to be understood in the auditorium. 9. (precise)
10. Smoking cigarettes may ...?... physical and mental growth. 10. (retard)

EXERCISE 6

Fill in the chart below with the Master Word that fits each set of clues. Part of speech refers to the word's usage in the lesson. Use a dictionary when necessary.

Number of Syllables	Part of Speech	Other Clues		Master Word
1	adjective	the Grand Canyon, for example	1.	(vast)
3	noun	where stars and clouds can be seen	2.	(firmament)
2	adjective	down to the last second	3.	(precise)
4	noun	dense fog creates this	4.	(opacity)
2	verb	a snowstorm can do this to travelers	5.	(retard)
1	noun	a stretch of land or identical houses, for example	6.	(tract)
1	noun	wasteland	7.	(heath)
2	adjective	an invalid might look this way	8.	(pallid)
4	adjective	from one step to the next	9.	(transitional)
3	verb	what you do when you brainstorm	10.	(generate)

LESSON 12

Part I: From the list below, choose the correct word for each sentence that follows. Use each word only once.

alleviate	consisted	futility	indelible
allusion	entitle	impetuous	surge
chafe	ferocity	imprecation	transitional

1. The senator made (a, an) ___(allusion)___ to an oft-quoted passage from Shakespeare.
2. Because it was Nola's birthday, the dinner ___(consisted)___ of all her favorite foods.
3. At the bell the boxers resumed fighting with undiminished ___(ferocity)___ in the savage contest.
4. He came to regret his ___(impetuous)___ action, later after he had taken the time to reconstruct the situation calmly.
5. When the power was turned back on, a ___(surge)___ of electricity caused her computer to crash.
6. This salve should ___(alleviate)___ at least temporarily the pain caused by the burn.
7. The cold wind had ___(chafe)___ (d, ed) the child's face, causing large, red blotches.
8. The angry citizen hurled (a, an) ___(imprecation)___ at the council members who had knowingly committed such an irresponsible and disastrous act.
9. For a few months after a new president takes over, the government is in (a, an) ___(transitional)___ stage.
10. Trying to keep the snowman from melting in 60 degree weather was an exercise in ___(futility)___.
11. Meeting the Dalai Lama left a(n) ___(indelible)___ impression on the students.
12. Mr. Fine's only living relative, Hannah was ___(entitle)___ (d, ed) to a share of his estate.

Part II: From the list below, choose the correct word for each sentence that follows. Use each word only once.

ambitious	dispel	generate	retort
concepts	diversity	ingenuity	sarcastic
derive	facilitate	obliterate	subjugation

1. The brilliant solution he eventually arrived at was typical of the ___(ingenuity)___ he always displayed in solving problems.
2. He responded to the unreasonable accusation with an angry, curt ___(retort)___.
3. I was asked what benefit I expected to ___(derive)___ from the planned course of action.
4. Many people tend to think that all monkeys are alike, but the family of apes contains a great ___(diversity)___ of these creatures.

5. The tribe remained in ____(subjugation)____ to the Spanish conquerors for thirty years.

6. That the universe may continue "forever" is one of those ____(concepts)____ that is difficult to grasp.

7. Hitler tried ruthlessly to ____(obliterate) (dispel)____ opposition to his plans for world domination.

8. A carefully planned and executed campaign ____(generate)____ (d, ed) a high level of public interest in the new plan.

9. The director's assurances failed to ____(dispel) (obliterate)____ the cast's opening-night jitters.

10. She immediately regretted her ____(sarcastic)____ remark, once she realized how much it had hurt his feelings.

EXERCISE 4

Part III: Decide whether the first pair in the items below are synonyms or antonyms. Then choose a Master Word from Lessons 1–11 that shows a similar relation to the word(s) preceding the blank. Do not repeat a Master Word that appears in the first column.

1. succor	:air	::sneer	: (taunt)
2. saunter	:march	::civility	: (savagery)
3. eclipse	:trail	::disregard	: (recollect)
4. proffered	:tendered	::peaceful	: (tranquil)
5. solace	:torment	::rosy	: (pallid)
6. curious	:odd	::acquire	: (procure)
7. perturbation	:peace of mind	::destroyed	: (erected)
8. compel	:release	::inexact	: (precise)
9. altruism	:selfishness	::murky	: (patent)
10. staid	:serious	::hope	: (expectancy)
11. knitted	:wrinkled	::filthy	: (grimy)
12. concur	:agree	::cloudiness	: (opacity)
13. ascend	:rise	::start	: (institute)
14. ambitious	:lazy	::opening	: (termination)
15. expedient	:inconvenience	::encased	: (sprawling)
16. haphazardly	:randomly	::ambition	: (initiative)
17. bestow	:withhold	::withdrawal	: (deposit)
18. pulverize	:demolish	::reduce	: (alleviate)
19. sanitary facilities	:toilets	::curse	: (revile)
20. indelible	:forgettable	::loot	: (endow)

LESSON **13**

Read the following selection to get the general meaning. Read it a second time, paying special attention to the words in dark type. Notice how they are used in sentences. These are Master Words. These are the words you will be working with in this section.

from ***The Joy Luck Club***
by Amy Tan

My mother started the San Francisco **version** of the Joy Luck Club in 1949, two years before I was born. This was the year my mother and father left China with one stiff leather trunk filled only with fancy silk dresses. There was no time to pack anything else, my mother had explained to my father after they boarded the boat. Still his hands swam **frantically** between the slippery silks, looking for his cotton shirts and wool pants.

When they arrived in San Francisco, my father made her hide those shiny clothes. She wore the same brown-checked Chinese dress until the **Refugee** Welcome Society gave her two hand-me-down dresses, all too large in sizes for American women. The society was **composed** of a group of white-haired American **missionary** ladies from the First Chinese Baptist Church. And because of their gifts, my parents could not refuse their invitation to join the church. Nor could they ignore the old ladies' **practical** advice to improve their English through Bible study class on Wednesday nights and, later, through choir practice on Saturday mornings. This was how my parents met the Hsus, the Jongs, and the St. Clairs. My mother could sense that the women of these families also had **unspeakable** tragedies they had left behind in China and hopes they couldn't begin to **express** in their **fragile** English. Or at least, my mother recognized the **numbness** in these women's faces. And she saw how quickly their eyes moved when she told them her idea for the Joy Luck Club.

EXERCISE 1

SELF-TEST: After reading the above selection, do the following. Look at the Master Words below. Underline the words that you think you know. Circle the words that you are less sure about. Draw a square around the words you don't recognize.

MASTER WORDS

composed	**numbness**
express	**practical**
fragile	**refugee**
frantically	**unspeakable**
missionary	**version**

EXERCISE 2

Read the selection on the preceding page again, this time paying special attention to the ten Master Words. In the (a) spaces provided below, write down what you think is the meaning of the word. After you have attempted a definition for each word, look up the word in a dictionary. In the (b) spaces, copy the appropriate dictionary definition.

1. **composed** (v.)

   a. ____________________

   b. made up

2. **express** (v.)

   a. ____________________

   b. represent in words; convey

3. **fragile** (adj.)

   a. ____________________

   b. easily broken; weak

4. **frantically** (adv.)

   a. ____________________

   b. marked by fast, nervous activity; anxiously

5. **missionary** (adj.)

   a. ____________________

   b. involved in humanitarian or conversion work for a religion

6. **numbness** (n.)

   a. ____________________

   b. lack of emotion or expression

7. **practical** (adj.)

   a. ____________________

   b. related to action rather than theory; sensible; useful

8. **refugee** (adj.)

   a. ____________________

   b. one who flees a country or power to avoid persecution

9. **unspeakable** (adj.)

   a. ____________________

   b. too awful to put into words; horrible

10. **version** (n.)

    a. ____________________

    b. form or variant of an original; adaptation

EXERCISE 3

Use the following list of synonyms and antonyms to fill in the blanks. Some of the words have no antonyms. In such cases, the antonym blanks have been marked with an X.

adaptation	conceal	horrible	original	useful
anxiously	convey	insensitivity	pleasing	useless
awareness	emigrant	made up	strong	weak
calmly	evangelist			

	Synonyms	**Antonyms**
1. **version**	(adaptation)	(original)
2. **frantically**	(anxiously)	(calmly)
3. **refugee**	(emigrant)	X
4. **composed**	(made up)	X
5. **missionary**	(evangelist)	X
6. **practical**	(useful)	(useless)
7. **unspeakable**	(horrible)	(pleasing)
8. **express**	(convey)	(conceal)
9. **fragile**	(weak)	(strong)
10. **numbness**	(insensitivity)	(awareness)

EXERCISE 4

Decide whether the first pair in the items below are synonyms or antonyms. Then choose the Master Word that shows a similar relation to the word(s) preceding the blank.

1. palatable	:offensive	::sturdy	: (fragile)
2. naturally	:instinctively	::put into words	: (convey)
3. thrill	:excitement	::sensible	: (practical)
4. random	:unplanned	::made up	: (composed)
5. forsake	:leave behind	::nervously	: (frantically)
6. minimize	:maximize	::original	: (version)
7. fastidious	:sloppy	::sensitivity	: (numbness)
8. provide	:deprive	::pleasing	: (unspeakable)
9. conquer	:subjugate	::evangelist	: (missionary)
10. obligated	:required	::asylum seeker	: (refugee)

EXERCISE 5

The Master Words in this lesson are repeated below. From the Master Words, choose the appropriate word for the blank in each of the following sentences. Write the word in the numbered space provided at the right.

composed	fragile	missionary	practical	unspeakable
convey	frantically	numbness	refugee	version

1. The kind ...?... couple opened a free medical clinic next to the church. — 1. (missionary)
2. The pain from the wound soon lessened into a reassuring ...?... . — 2. (numbness)
3. She was introverted and shy, so it was difficult for her to ...?... her feelings in front of a crowd. — 3. (convey)
4. The film ...?... of this famous Broadway play didn't live up to the promotional hype. — 4. (version)
5. The ...?... families were relieved to have escaped the danger at home, but nervous about what awaited them in their new country. — 5. (refugee)
6. The butterfly's wings seemed so ...?..., yet she knew they would carry the creature far on its migratory flight. — 6. (fragile)
7. The creative writing club was ...?... of an interesting mix of brainy, artsy, and athletic students. — 7. (composed)
8. What started out as a simple prank had turned into (a, an) ...?... horror. — 8. (unspeakable)
9. She was tired of all this theory and ready to learn some ...?... applications. — 9. (practical)
10. As the fire rose in the sky, wild animals careened ...?... out of the woods. — 10. (frantically)

EXERCISE 6

Using one of the Master Words, create an acrostic composition related to the meaning of the word. See the example below.

Retreat!
Enough
Fear,
InjUstice.
BeGin
anEw.
HopE!

(Answers will vary. See example in lesson.)

LESSON 14

Read the following selection to get the general meaning. Read it a second time, paying special attention to the words in dark type. Notice how they are used in sentences. These are Master Words. These are the words you will be working with in this lesson.

From **Cranford**
by Elizabeth Cleghorn Gaskell

It was impossible to live a month at Cranford and not know the daily habits of each resident; and long before my visit was ended, I knew much concerning the whole Brown trio. There was nothing new to be discovered respecting their poverty; for they had spoken simply and openly about that from the very first. They made no mystery of the necessity for their being **economical**. All that remained to be discovered was the Captain's **infinite** kindness of heart, and the various **modes** in which, **unconsciously** to himself, he manifested it. Some little **anecdotes** were talked about for some time after they occurred. As we did not read much, and as all the ladies were pretty well suited with servants, there was a **dearth** of subjects for conversation. We therefore discussed the circumstance of the Captain taking a poor old woman's dinner out of her hands, one very slippery Sunday. He had met her returning from the bakehouse as he came from church and noticed her **precarious** footing; and, with the **grave** dignity with which he did everything, he **relieved** her of her burden, and **steered** along the street by her side, carrying her baked mutton and potatoes safely home.

EXERCISE 1

SELF-TEST: After reading the above selection, do the following. Look at the Master Words below. Underline the words that you think you know. Circle the words that you are less sure about. Draw a square around the words you don't recognize.

MASTER WORDS

anecdote	**mode**
dearth	**precarious**
economical	**relieve**
grave	**steer**
infinite	**unconscious**

EXERCISE 2

Read the selection on the preceding page again, this time paying special attention to the ten Master Words. In the (a) spaces provided below, write down what you think is the meaning of the word. After you have attempted a definition for each word, look up the word in a dictionary. In the (b) spaces, copy the appropriate dictionary definition.

1. **anecdote** (n.)

   a. ______

   b. a small story, usually entertaining and frequently amusing; a short account

2. **dearth** (n.)

   a. ______

   b. lack; scarcity; shortage

3. **economical** (adj.)

   a. ______

   b. frugal; thrifty; not wasteful

4. **grave** (adj.)

   a. ______

   b. somber; dignified

5. **infinite** (adj.)

   a. ______

   b. without limits; unbounded; endless

6. **mode** (n.)

   a. ______

   b. manner; method; custom; form

7. **precarious** (adj.)

   a. ______

   b. not certain; delicately in balance; suggesting danger

8. **relieve** (v.)

   a. ______

   b. to free from burden; to remove a pressure

9. **steer** (v.)

   a. ______

   b. to direct the course of; to pilot

10. **unconscious** (adj.)

   a. ______

   b. unaware; involuntary

EXERCISE 3

Use the following list of synonyms and antonyms to fill in the blanks.

abundance	epic	lighthearted	secure
boundless	exception	limited	solemn
custom	extravagant	mindful	story
drift	frugal	overload	unaware
ease	guide	scarcity	unstable

	Synonyms	**Antonyms**
1. **economical**	(frugal)	(extravagant)
2. **infinite**	(boundless)	(limited)
3. **mode**	(custom)	(exception)
4. **unconscious**	(unaware)	(mindful)
5. **anecdote**	(story)	(epic)
6. **dearth**	(scarcity)	(abundance)
7. **precarious**	(unstable)	(secure)
8. **grave**	(solemn)	(lighthearted)
9. **relieve**	(ease)	(overload)
10. **steer**	(guide)	(drift)

EXERCISE 4

Decide whether the first pair in the items below are synonyms or antonyms. Then choose the Master Word that shows a similar relation to the word(s) preceding the blank.

1. behold	:view	::manner	: (mode)
2. prehistoric	:new	::steady	: (precarious)
3. weary	:refreshed	::strain	: (relieve)
4. brace	:strengthen	::pilot	: (steer)
5. vagrant	:resident	::knowing	: (unconscious)
6. fragile	:unbreakable	::measurable	: (infinite)
7. exception	:norm	::cheerful	: (grave)
8. exhibit	:display	::thrifty	: (economical)
9. elongate	:stretch	::lack	: (dearth)
10. annual	:yearly	::tale	: (anecdote)

EXERCISE 5

The Master Words in this lesson are repeated below. From the Master Words, choose the appropriate word for the blank in each of the following sentences. Write the word in the numbered space provided at the right.

anecdote	economical	infinite	precarious	steer
dearth	grave	mode	relieve	unconscious

1. Generally, consumers find it more ...?... to purchase products in larger packages. — 1. (economical)
2. The Prime Minister was ...?... as he announced the assassination of the Grand Duke. — 2. (grave)
3. Coaches complain that there is (a, an) ...?... of large, agile linemen. — 3. (dearth)
4. The concept of the ...?... is bounded only by the human imagination. — 4. (infinite)
5. A small ...?..., well told, can serve to instruct as well as entertain. — 5. (anecdote)
6. The ...?... of dress changes so quickly one is discouraged from spending large sums on clothing. — 6. (mode)
7. To ...?... a car is not really to drive it. — 7. (steer)
8. Some people say that forgetting is the ...?... fulfillment of a wish. — 8. (unconscious)
9. Modern medicine offers many ways to ...?... pain. — 9. (relieve)
10. The early pioneers lived (a, an) ...?... existence, subject to the whims of natural disaster as well as threats from wild animals. — 10. (precarious)

EXERCISE 6

To complete the word spiral, choose the Master Word associated with each phrase below. Start with 1 and fill in each answer clockwise. Be careful! Each new word may overlap the previous word by one or more letters.

1. very short story
2. aspirin may do this
3. a serious situation, for instance
4. style or way of doing something
5. endangered species are an example of this
6. reflexes, for example
7. a person at the helm does this
8. like footing on a tightrope, for example
9. describes the number of times you can cross a line
10. smaller cars are usually this

1. A	N	E	C	D	O	T	E
N	C	O	N	S	C	I	2. R
6. U	U	S	9. I	N	F	O	E
H	O	M	I	C	I	U	L
T	I	O		A	N	7. S	I
R	R	N		L	I	T	E
A	A	O	C	10. E	T	E	V
E	C	E	R	8. P	R	E	E
5. D	O	4. M	E	V	A	R	3. G

LESSON 15

Read the following selection to get the general meaning. Read it a second time, paying special attention to the words in dark type. Notice how they are used in sentences. These are Master Words. These are the words you will be working with in this lesson.

From **The Chimes**
by Charles Dickens

For the night-wind has a **dismal** trick of wandering round and round a building of that sort, and moaning as it goes; and of trying, with its unseen hand, the windows and the doors; and seeking out some **crevices** by which to enter. And when it has got in, as one not finding what it seeks, whatever that may be, it wails and howls to issue forth again: and not content with stalking through the aisles, and gliding round and round the pillars, and tempting the deep organ, soars up to the roof, and **strives** to rend the rafters: then flings itself **despairingly** upon the stones below, and passes, muttering, into the **vaults**. Anon, it comes up **stealthily**, and creeps along the walls, seeming to read, in whispers, the Inscriptions sacred to the Dead. At some of these, it breaks out **shrilly**, as with laughter; and at others, moans and cries as if it were **lamenting**. It has a ghostly sound too, lingering within the altar; where it seems to chant, in its wild way, of Wrong and Murder done, and false Gods worshipped, in **defiance** of the Tables of the Law, which look so fair and smooth, but are so **flawed** and broken.

EXERCISE 1

SELF-TEST: After reading the above selection, do the following. Look at the Master Words below. Underline the words that you think you know. Circle the words that you are less sure about. Draw a square around the words you don't recognize.

MASTER WORDS	
crevice	**lament**
defiance	**shrill**
despairingly	**stealthily**
dismal	**strive**
flawed	**vault**

EXERCISE 2

Read the selection on the preceding page again, this time paying special attention to the ten Master Words. In the (a) spaces provided below, write down what you think is the meaning of the word. After you have attempted a definition for each word, look up the word in a dictionary. In the (b) spaces, copy the appropriate dictionary definition.

1. **crevice** (n.)

   a. ______________________

   b. a narrow opening; a crack

2. **defiance** (n.)

   a. ______________________

   b. resistance; challenge

3. **despairingly** (adv.)

   a. ______________________

   b. hopelessly; despondently

4. **dismal** (adj.)

   a. ______________________

   b. gloomy and cheerless

5. **flawed** (adj.)

   a. ______________________

   b. damaged; defective; imperfect

6. **lament** (v.)

   a. ______________________

   b. to express deep regret; to grieve

7. **shrill** (adj.)

   a. ______________________

   b. sharp and high-pitched, as a shriek; piercing

8. **stealthily** (adv.)

   a. ______________________

   b. slyly; secretively; furtively

9. **strive** (v.)

   a. ______________________

   b. to work hard; to labor; to seek a goal energetically

10. **vault** (n.)

    a. ______________________

    b. a burial chamber; a tomb

EXERCISE 3

Use the following list of synonyms and antonyms to fill in the blanks. Some words have no antonyms. In such cases, the antonym blanks have been marked with an X.

acceptance	dreary	marred	rejoice
bemoan	filling	openly	struggle
cheerful	furtively	perfect	tomb
cranny	hopefully	piercing	tuneful
despondently	loaf	rebellion	

	Synonyms	Antonyms
1. **dismal**	(dreary)	(cheerful)
2. **crevice**	(cranny)	(filling)
3. **strive**	(struggle)	(loaf)
4. **despairingly**	(despondently)	(hopefully)
5. **vault**	(tomb)	X
6. **lament**	(bemoan)	(rejoice)
7. **stealthily**	(furtively)	(openly)
8. **shrill**	(piercing)	(tuneful)
9. **defiance**	(rebellion)	(acceptance)
10. **flawed**	(marred)	(perfect)

EXERCISE 4

Decide whether the first pair in the items below are synonyms or antonyms. Then choose the Master Word that shows a similar relation to the word(s) preceding the blank.

1. anecdote	:story	::crack	: (crevice)
2. steer	:direct	::labor	: (strive)
3. economical	:wasteful	::tolerance	: (defiance)
4. mode	:method	::sharp	: (shrill)
5. infinite	:unlimited	::hopelessly	: (despairingly)
6. dearth	:surplus	::delight	: (lament)
7. grave	:jolly	::merry	: (dismal)
8. unconscious	:unmindful	::mausoleum	: (vault)
9. precarious	:stable	::undefective	: (flawed)
10. relieve	:burden	::publicly	: (stealthily)

EXERCISE 5

The Master Words in this lesson are repeated below. From the Master Words, choose the appropriate word for the blank in each of the following sentences. Write the word in the numbered space provided at the right.

crevice	despairingly	flawed	shrill	strive
defiance	dismal	lament	stealthily	vault

1. The ...?... voices of the girls could be heard above the usual pre-assembly auditorium sounds. 1. (shrill)
2. The jewel thief moved ...?... through the house, so quietly that not a stair creaked. 2. (stealthily)
3. No one will criticize if you ...?... to meet your goals, even though you may be imperfect. 3. (strive)
4. The ...?... of a lonely heron who had lost his mate echoed across the water. 4. (lament)
5. The team worked ...?... to get a touchdown, even after four quarters without scoring. 5. (despairingly)
6. One rule of anarchy is reckless ...?... of established conventions. 6. (defiance)
7. Along the mountainside, flowers grew in (a, an) ...?... by the stream. 7. (crevice)
8. The young candidate believed he had made (a, an) ...?... showing, since he had won only two of twenty-four precincts. 8. (dismal)
9. Only because the diamond was slightly ...?... did it fail to bring the record price. 9. (flawed)
10. Distinguished artists, writers, and scholars were frequently buried in the ...?... at the medieval church. 10. (vault)

EXERCISE 6

Use at least five Master Words from this lesson to write a scene about one of the following topics. Or create a topic of your own. Write your choice on the blank. Circle the Master Words as you use them.

Possible Topics: Graveyard Scare, Down in the Dungeon

(Note: Answers will vary.)

LESSON 16

Read the following selection to get the general meaning. Read it a second time, paying special attention to the words in dark type. Notice how they are used in sentences. These are Master Words. These are the words you will be working with in this section.

from ***Black Ice***
by Lorene Cary

I could see them from the **dais**: families and friends sitting on the **risers**, young students spilling out onto the grass, black-robed faculty members standing in front of their seats—all watching for the first graduates to begin their march down the grassy aisle between the folding chairs on the **green**. Someone let out a **whoop** as they appeared, the girls in their white dresses and the boys in their jackets and ties.

Fifteen years before, I had walked down the same aisle as a graduate, and nine years later as a teacher. Now I was ending my term as a **trustee**.

I watched the black and Hispanic students, "my kids," come to the **podium** to receive their diplomas and awards from the Rector. One young man named Harlem winked at me as he passed. His shoulders still rocked a little, just a little, like the shoulders of black men in cities, and he held himself up on the balls of his feet like the ballet dancer he had become while at St. Paul's School. I remembered him as a Fourth Former, his head **cocked** to one side, asking, "I'd like to know: would you send *your* daughter to St. Paul's?"

The other students had laughed in that way that teenagers do when an adult is forced to reveal herself. But we also laughed together as black people alone, safe for the moment within the group, the collective tensions and **harmonic** humor of it, relieved for an hour or so from our **headlong** rush toward individual **achievement**.

"My daughter will have to decide that for herself," I said. "Don't roll your eyes. I mean it. My parents did not make me come here. I was bound and determined. They *let* me, and it was not an easy thing to do."

EXERCISE 1

SELF-TEST: After reading the above selection, do the following. Look at the Master Words below. Underline the words that you think you know. Circle the words that you are less sure about. Draw a square around the words you don't recognize.

MASTER WORDS	
achievement	**headlong**
cocked	**podium**
dais	**risers**
green	**trustee**
harmonic	**whoop**

EXERCISE 2

Read the selection on the preceding page again, this time paying special attention to the ten Master Words. In the (a) spaces provided below, write down what you think is the meaning of the word. After you have attempted a definition for each word, look up the word in a dictionary. In the (b) spaces, copy the appropriate dictionary definition.

1. **achievement** (n.)

   a. ____________________

   b. result gained by effort; accomplishment

2. **cocked** (adj.)

   a. ____________________

   b. turned to one side; tilted

3. **dais** (n.)

   a. ____________________

   b. raised platform in a hall or large room

4. **green** (n.)

   a. ____________________

   b. grassy park or lawn

5. **harmonic** (adj.)

   a. ____________________

   b. understood; resonant; congenial

6. **headlong** (adj.)

   a. ____________________

   b. reckless; without pause for thought

7. **podium** (n.)

   a. ____________________

   b. speaker's stand; lectern

8. **risers** (n.)

   a. ____________________

   b. stage platforms designed to make groups of performers visible

9. **trustee** (n.)

   a. ____________________

   b. one to whom something is entrusted; board member

10. **whoop** (n.)

    a. ____________________

    b. exuberant shout

EXERCISE 3

Use the following list of synonyms and antonyms to fill in the blanks. Some of the words have no antonyms. In such cases, the antonym blanks have been marked with an X.

accomplishment	disturbing	impetuous	platform	straight
board member	failure	lawn	shout	tilted
congenial	hesitant	lectern	steps	whisper

	Synonyms	Antonyms
1. **dais**	(platform)	X
2. **risers**	(steps)	X
3. **green**	(lawn)	X
4. **whoop**	(shout)	(whisper)
5. **trustee**	(board member)	X
6. **podium**	(lectern)	X
7. **cocked**	(tilted)	(straight)
8. **harmonic**	(congenial)	(disturbing)
9. **headlong**	(impetuous)	(hesitant)
10. **achievement**	(accomplishment)	(failure)

EXERCISE 4

Decide whether the first pair in the items below are synonyms or antonyms. Then choose the Master Word that shows a similar relation to the word(s) preceding the blank.

1. faithful	:treacherous	::deliberate	: (headlong)
2. offspring	:descendants	::tipped	: (cocked)
3. plot	:conspiracy	::board member	: (trustee)
4. augment	:decrease	::failure	: (achievement)
5. demure	:rowdy	::disturbing	: (harmonic)
6. premise	:assumption	::lectern	: (podium)
7. execute	:enforce	::steps	: (risers)
8. loud	:raucous	::commons	: (green)
9. serene	:tumultuous	::whisper	: (whoop)
10. pattern	:template	::stage	: (dais)

EXERCISE 5

The Master Words in this lesson are repeated below. From the Master Words, choose the appropriate word for the blank in each of the following sentences. Write the word in the numbered space provided at the right.

achievement	dais	harmonic	podium	trustee
cocked	green	headlong	risers	whoop

1. Mrs. Harmon had been (a, an) ...?... and was later president of the library board. 1. (trustee)
2. Juan needed to think about his college choice before rushing ...?... into a decision. 2. (headlong)
3. It was (a, an) ...?... arrangement of items in the room; each item seemed to complement the others. 3. (harmonic)
4. The couple decided to hold the wedding on the village ...?... . 4. (green)
5. The lecturer took her place behind the ...?... and began the lesson. 5. (podium)
6. The bird's head was ...?... as though it heard a danger signal. 6. (cocked)
7. When her name was called her parents let out a joyous ...?... . 7. (whoop)
8. In honor of their ...?..., a plaque was installed in the auditorium. 8. (achievement)
9. Robert walked slowly toward the ...?... at the front of the room, aware that all eyes were on him. 9. (dais)
10. She could already feel the tears coming, and the choir was just filing onto the ...?... . 10. (risers)

EXERCISE 6

Anagrams: Choose three of the Master Words. Write one at the top of each blank column below. Underneath each Master Word, write all the words you can think of that are made up of letters found in the Master Word. See the example.

harmonic			
cram			
charm			
manic			
harm			
ran			
ham			
moan			
icon			
march			
in			

(Answers will vary. See example in lesson.)

LESSON 17

Read the following selection to get the general meaning. Read it a second time, paying special attention to the words in dark type. Notice how they are used in sentences. These are Master Words. These are the words you will be working with in this lesson.

From **Nightmare Abbey**
by Thomas Love Peacock

Nightmare Abbey, a **venerable** family-mansion, in a highly **picturesque** state of semi-**dilapidation**, pleasantly situated on a strip of dry land between the sea and the fens at the **verge** of the county of Lincoln, had the honor to be the seat of Christopher Glowry, Esquire. This gentleman was naturally of an atrabilarious [this word, meaning gloomy, was coined by Peacock] **temperament**. . . . He had been deceived in an early friendship: he had been crossed in love; he had offered his land, from **pique**, to a lady, who accepted it from interest, and who, in so doing, violently tore asunder the bonds of a tried and youthful attachment. Her vanity was gratified by being the mistress of a very extensive, if not very lively establishment; but all the springs of her sympathies were frozen. Riches she possessed, but that which enriches them, the **participation** of affection, was wanting. All that they could purchase for her became **indifferent** to her, because that which they could not purchase, and which was more valuable than themselves, she had, for their sake, thrown away. She discovered, when it was too late, that she had mistaken the means for the end—that riches, rightly used, are instruments of happiness, but are not in themselves happiness. In this wilful **blight** of her affections, she found them valueless as means: they had been the end to which she had **immolated** all her affections, and were not the only end that remained to her.

EXERCISE 1

SELF-TEST: After reading the above selection, do the following. Look at the Master Words below. Underline the words that you think you know. Circle the words that you are less sure about. Draw a square around the words you don't recognize.

MASTER WORDS

blight	**picturesque**
dilapidation	**pique**
immolate	**temperament**
indifferent	**venerable**
participation	**verge**

EXERCISE 2

Read the selection on the preceding page again, this time paying special attention to the ten Master Words. In the (a) spaces provided below, write down what you think is the meaning of the word. After you have attempted a definition for each word, look up the word in a dictionary. In the (b) spaces, copy the appropriate dictionary definition.

1. **blight** (n.)
   a. ______
   b. decline; decay; ruin; withering
2. **dilapidation** (n.)
   a. ______
   b. condition of rot or disrepair
3. **immolate** (v.)
   a. ______
   b. to sacrifice
4. **indifferent** (adj.)
   a. ______
   b. unaware; insensitive; cold; unresponsive
5. **participation** (n.)
   a. ______
   b. sharing with others; involvement of self
6. **picturesque** (adj.)
   a. ______
   b. charming; strikingly unusual; suitable for a picture
7. **pique** (n.)
   a. ______
   b. anger or resentment
8. **temperament** (n.)
   a. ______
   b. mental and physical character of a person
9. **venerable** (adj.)
   a. ______
   b. worthy of reverence and respect
10. **verge** (n.)
    a. ______
    b. border; limit; margin; edge

EXERCISE 3

Use the following list of synonyms and antonyms to fill in the blanks. Some words have no antonyms. In such cases, the antonym blanks have been marked with an X.

bloom	disposition	resentment	soundness
center	edge	ruin	spiritlessness
contemptible	friendliness	sacrifice	unsightly
cool	friendly	save	withdrawal
decay	involvement	scenic	worthy

	Synonyms	**Antonyms**
1. **picturesque**	(scenic)	(unsightly)
2. **dilapidation**	(decay) (ruin)	(soundness)
3. **venerable**	(worthy)	(contemptible)
4. **verge**	(edge)	(center)
5. **temperament**	(disposition)	(spiritlessness)
6. **pique**	(resentment)	(friendliness)
7. **participation**	(involvement)	(withdrawal)
8. **indifferent**	(cool)	(friendly)
9. **blight**	(ruin) (decay)	(bloom)
10. **immolate**	(sacrifice)	(save)

EXERCISE 4

Decide whether the first pair in the items below are synonyms or antonyms. Then choose the Master Word that shows a similar relation to the word(s) preceding the blank.

1. procedure	:approach	::kill	: (immolate)
2. approbation	:objection	::despised	: (venerable)
3. gratify	:annoy	::pleasantness	: (pique)
4. proprietor	:owner	::nature	: (temperament)
5. undisputed	:debatable	::isolation	: (participation)
6. uniform	:varied	::ugly	: (picturesque)
7. chamber	:room	::withering	: (blight)
8. motive	:reason	::disrepair	: (dilapidation)
9. sole	:single	::border	: (verge)
10. grandeur	:poverty	::interested	: (indifferent)

EXERCISE 5

The Master Words in this lesson are repeated below. From the Master Words, choose the appropriate word for the blank in each of the following sentences. Write the word in the numbered space provided at the right.

blight	immolate	participation	pique	venerable
dilapidation	indifferent	picturesque	temperament	verge

1. Shoe clerks must have an even ...?... if they are to keep their sanity. — 1. (temperament)
2. The highly publicized star gave only (a, an) ...?... performance for 10,000 disappointed fans. — 2. (indifferent)
3. In his ...?..., the shortstop threw the ball into the taunting crowd. — 3. (pique)
4. Tomato growers were afraid of the mysterious ...?... that was wilting the plants. — 4. (blight)
5. Their ...?... in the Gold Cup games was not certain. — 5. (participation)
6. Now ...?... was moving in on the proud, 100-year-old Victorian mansions on Tower Street. — 6. (dilapidation)
7. Some Orientals ...?... themselves by fire as a drastic expression of protest. — 7. (immolate)
8. The ...?... patriarch's wisdom was written with the gray hairs of his head. — 8. (venerable)
9. Currier and Ives' New England snow scenes make ...?... Christmas cards. — 9. (picturesque)
10. You can call the paper and tell them the committee is now on the ...?... of a decision. — 10. (verge)

EXERCISE 6

Write the Master Word that is associated with each word group below. Then list three things that might be associated with the review word that follows.

1. cool, passive, numb — (indifferent)
2. crops, Dust Bowl, potato — (blight)
3. landscape, postcard, garden — (picturesque)
4. peeling paint, falling plaster, condemned — (dilapidation)
5. volunteer, social, speak out — (participation)
6. artistic, high-strung, Type A — (temperament)
7. lamb, victims, crucify — (immolate)
8. cliff, tears, discovery — (verge)
9. scowl, red-faced, slow burn — (pique)
10. elder, redwoods, judge — (venerable)

Review word: steer (Lesson 14)

(pilot) (driver) (chauffeur)

(Note: Answers may vary.)

LESSON 18

Read the following selection to get the general meaning. Read it a second time, paying special attention to the words in dark type. Notice how they are used in sentences. These are Master Words. These are the words you will be working with in this lesson.

From **The House with the Green Shutters**
by George Douglas Brown

He was a man with mean brown eyes. Brown eyes may be clear and **limpid** as a mountain pool, or they may have the fine black flash of anger and the **jovial** gleam, or they may be mean things—little and **sly** and oily. Gibson's had the depth of cunning, not the depth of character, and they **glistened** like the eyes of a lustful animal. He was a reddish man, with a **fringe** of sandy beard, and a **perpetual** grin which showed his yellow teeth, with a green deposit round their roots. It was more than a grin . . . and the beady eyes, ever on the watch up above it, **belied** its false benevolence. He was not **florid**, yet that grin of his seemed to **intensify** his reddishness (perhaps because it brought out and made prominent . . . the **ruddy** round of his cheeks) so that the baker christened him long ago "the man with the sandy smile."

EXERCISE 1

SELF-TEST: After reading the above selection, do the following. Look at the Master Words below. Underline the words that you think you know. Circle the words that you are less sure about. Draw a square around the words you don't recognize.

MASTER WORDS

belie	**jovial**
florid	**limpid**
fringe	**perpetual**
glisten	**ruddy**
intensify	**sly**

EXERCISE 2

Read the selection on the preceding page again, this time paying special attention to the ten Master Words. In the (a) spaces provided below, write down what you think is the meaning of the word. After you have attempted a definition for each word, look up the word in a dictionary. In the (b) spaces, copy the appropriate dictionary definition.

1. **belie** (v.)
   a. ______
   b. to deceive; to tell an untruth; to misrepresent
2. **florid** (adj.)
   a. ______
   b. flushed; reddish
3. **fringe** (n.)
   a. ______
   b. a border or an edging of hair, strips of material, etc.; trimming
4. **glisten** (v.)
   a. ______
   b. to sparkle or shine
5. **intensify** (v.)
   a. ______
   b. to strengthen; to grow in density and feeling
6. **jovial** (adj.)
   a. ______
   b. hilarious; joyful; gaily spirited
7. **limpid** (adj.)
   a. ______
   b. clear or transparent
8. **perpetual** (adj.)
   a. ______
   b. uninterrupted; everlasting; indefinite
9. **ruddy** (adj.)
   a. ______
   b. red, usually from vigor, exposure, and good health
10. **sly** (adj.)
    a. ______
    b. artfully cunning; sneaky

EXERCISE 3

Use the following list of synonyms and antonyms to fill in the blanks. Some words have no antonyms. In such cases, the antonym blanks have been marked with an X.

center	darken	glitter	opaque
clear	deceive	increase	pale
continuous	diminish	inform	reddish
crafty	edging	jolly	rosy
crude	fleeting	morose	sallow

	Synonyms	Antonyms
1. **limpid**	(clear)	(opaque)
2. **jovial**	(jolly)	(morose)
3. **sly**	(crafty)	(crude)
4. **glisten**	(glitter)	(darken)
5. **fringe**	(edging)	(center)
6. **perpetual**	(continuous)	(fleeting)
7. **belie**	(deceive)	(inform)
8. **florid**	(rosy) (reddish)	(pale) (sallow)
9. **intensify**	(increase)	(diminish)
10. **ruddy**	(reddish) (rosy)	(sallow) (pale)

EXERCISE 4

Decide whether the first pair in the items below are synonyms or antonyms. Then choose the Master Word that shows a similar relation to the word(s) preceding the blank.

1. pique	:good will	::sad	: (jovial)
2. venerable	:unworthy	::cloud	: (glisten)
3. temperament	:character	::transparent	: (limpid)
4. blight	:destruction	::mislead	: (belie)
5. indifferent	:unconcerned	::strengthen	: (intensify)
6. verge	:brink	::flushed	: (ruddy) (florid)
7. dilapidation	:repair	::pallid	: (florid) (ruddy)
8. participation	:separation	::momentary	: (perpetual)
9. picturesque	:unattractive	::straightforward	: (sly)
10. immolate	:sacrifice	::trimming	: (fringe)

EXERCISE 5

The Master Words in this lesson are repeated below. From the Master Words, choose the appropriate word for the blank in each of the following sentences. Write the word in the numbered space provided at the right.

belie	fringe	intensify	limpid	ruddy
florid	glisten	jovial	perpetual	sly

1. His frequent flashes of anger ...?... his true good nature. 1. (belie)
2. There is ...?... light at the tomb of the Unknown Soldier. 2. (perpetual)
3. As Christmas Eve approaches, feelings of good will and peace seem to ...?... . 3. (intensify)
4. The camping trip brought (a, an) ...?... color to Kevin's normally pale face. 4. (ruddy) (florid)
5. In the ...?... stream he watched the silver trout swish about. 5. (limpid)
6. The kitchen hummed with ...?... chatter as the family gathered to prepare the feast. 6. (jovial)
7. The turn-of-the-century surreys had ...?... around the top. 7. (fringe)
8. His ...?... face, familiar around the lodge, testified to his love of skiing. 8. (florid) (ruddy)
9. Adding (a, an) ...?... fake to his regular "square-out" pattern, Roger caught the ball easily in the end zone. 9. (sly)
10. What Mark Twain saw ...?... in the dim light was mica, not gold. 10. (glisten)

EXERCISE 6

To complete the crossword, choose the Master Word associated with each word or phrase below. Begin each answer in the square having the same number as the clue.

1. sailor's face, perhaps
2. like Santa Claus' behavior
3. like time or change
4. turn up the volume
5. often found on a shawl
6. flushed
7. like clear streams
8. distort like a fun house mirror
9. snowflakes do this in moonlight
10. like a fox

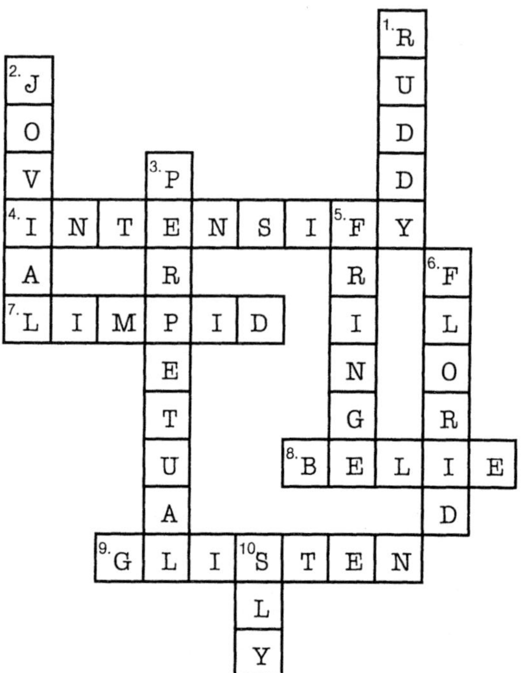

LESSON 19

Read the following selection to get the general meaning. Read it a second time, paying special attention to the words in dark type. Notice how they are used in sentences. These are Master Words. These are the words you will be working with in this lesson.

From **Autobiography of Mark Rutherford**
by William Hale White

But my thoughts turned almost immediately to myself, and I could bring myself to no **resolve**. I was weak and tired, and the more I thought the less **capable** was I of coming to my decision. In the morning, after a restless night, I was in still greater **straits**, and being perfectly unable to do anything, I fled to my usual refuge, the sea. The whole day I swayed to and fro, without the smallest power to **arbitrate** between the **contradictory impulses** which drew me in opposite directions. I knew what I ought to do, but Ellen's image was ever before me, **mutely** appealing against her wrongs, and I pictured her deserted and with her life spoiled. I said to myself that **instinct** is all very well, but for what purpose is reason given to us if not to reason with it, and reasoning in the main is a correction of what is called instinct, and of hasty first impressions . . . I came home thoroughly beaten with **fatigue**. Fortunately I sank at once to rest, and with the morning was born the clear **discernment** that whatever I ought to do, it was more manly of me to go than to write to Ellen. Accordingly, I made arrangements for getting somebody to supply my place in the pulpit for a couple of Sundays, and went home.

EXERCISE 1

SELF-TEST: After reading the above selection, do the following. Look at the Master Words below. Underline the words that you think you know. Circle the words that you are less sure about. Draw a square around the words you don't recognize.

MASTER WORDS

arbitrate	**impulse**
capable	**instinct**
contradictory	**mute**
discernment	**resolve**
fatigue	**straits**

EXERCISE 2

Read the selection on the preceding page again, this time paying special attention to the ten Master Words. In the (a) spaces provided below, write down what you think is the meaning of the word. After you have attempted a definition for each word, look up the word in a dictionary. In the (b) spaces, copy the appropriate dictionary definition.

1. **arbitrate** (v.)
   a. ______
   b. to decide or determine; to make a judgment

2. **capable** (adj.)
   a. ______
   b. competent; fit to perform a task

3. **contradictory** (adj.)
   a. ______
   b. opposing; inconsistent; on the contrary; against the grain

4. **discernment** (n.)
   a. ______
   b. perception; recognition; detection

5. **fatigue** (n.)
   a. ______
   b. weariness from labor or exertion; exhaustion

6. **impulse** (n.)
   a. ______
   b. force; urge; inclination; tendency; motive

7. **instinct** (n.)
   a. ______
   b. a natural tendency; unlearned behavior

8. **mute** (adj.)
   a. ______
   b. unspeaking; not uttered; silent

9. **resolve** (n.)
   a. ______
   b. determination; firmness of purpose; intent

10. **straits** (n.)
    a. ______
    b. distress; confusion; difficulty

EXERCISE 3

Use the following list of synonyms and antonyms to fill in the blanks. Some words have no antonyms. In such cases, the antonym blanks have been marked with an X.

agreeable	easiness	mediate	spontaneity
competent	imperception	opposing	uncertainty
determination	inept	perception	vigor
difficulty	insensitivity	rehearsal	vocal
dispute	intuition	silent	weariness

	Synonyms	Antonyms
1. **resolve**	(determination)	(uncertainty)
2. **capable**	(competent)	(inept)
3. **straits**	(difficulty)	(easiness)
4. **arbitrate**	(mediate)	(dispute)
5. **contradictory**	(opposing)	(agreeable)
6. **impulse**	(spontaneity)	(rehearsal)
7. **mute**	(silent)	(vocal)
8. **instinct**	(intuition)	(imperception) (insensitivity)
9. **fatigue**	(weariness)	(vigor)
10. **discernment**	(perception)	(insensitivity) (imperception)

EXERCISE 4

Decide whether the first pair in the items below are synonyms or antonyms. Then choose the Master Word that shows a similar relation to the word(s) preceding the blank.

1. fringe	:border	::insight	: (instinct)
2. glisten	:dull	::dispute	: (arbitrate)
3. ruddy	:blushing	::trouble	: (straits)
4. intensify	:weaken	::incompetent	: (capable)
5. perpetual	:temporary	::energy	: (fatigue)
6. sly	:forthright	::talkative	: (mute)
7. belie	:misrepresent	::understanding	: (discernment)
8. limpid	:crystal	::firmness	: (resolve)
9. florid	:reddish	::urge	: (impulse) (instinct)
10. jovial	:melancholy	::consistent	: (contradictory)

EXERCISE 5

The Master Words in this lesson are repeated below. From the Master Words, choose the appropriate word for the blank in each of the following sentences. Write the word in the numbered space provided at the right.

arbitrate	contradictory	fatigue	instinct	resolve
capable	discernment	impulse	mute	straits

1. Our ...?... was to save money, so we skipped the movie. — 1. (resolve)
2. The umpire was called in to ...?... the close call at first base. — 2. (arbitrate)
3. Jack London believed that animal ...?... was superior to man's reason. — 3. (instinct)
4. Recklessly, Johnson decided on ...?... to jump from the plane. — 4. (impulse)
5. Everyone in the shop recognized him as a skilled mechanic, ...?... of handling the most delicate engine. — 5. (capable)
6. Failure to file the report may place us in severe financial ...?..., since our check will be tied up for weeks. — 6. (straits)
7. The defense attorney cited ...?... testimony from a previous witness, although he charged no one with perjury. — 7. (contradictory)
8. The frightened child remained ...?... in spite of the gentle questioning by the police. — 8. (mute)
9. A talent scout is responsible for the ...?... of people who can perform with grace and assurance. — 9. (discernment)
10. Vigorous exercise can result in ...?... . — 10. (fatigue)

EXERCISE 6

The invented words below are formed from parts of different Master Words from this lesson. Create a definition and indicate the part of speech for each word. The first one is done for you.

resolbitrate *(v.) to settle with determination*

impulstraits ([n.] trouble resulting from acting on a whim)

fatistraits ([n.] difficult situations that wear you out)

mutesolve ([n.] quiet determination)

Now invent your own words by combining parts of the Master Words. Create a definition for each, and indicate the word's part of speech. (You may reuse any of the word parts above in new combinations.)

1. ________ ________

2. ________ ________

(Note: Answers will vary.)

Other possibilities:
capamute (adj.) able to be silenced
straitsfatigue (n.) weariness resulting from being in a difficult position
impulstinct (n.) a tendency or inclination over which one has little control

LESSON 20

Read the following selection to get the general meaning. Read it a second time, paying special attention to the words in dark type. Notice how they are used in sentences. These are Master Words. These are the words you will be working with in this lesson.

From **Dr. Jekyll and Mr. Hyde**
by Robert Louis Stevenson

It was late in the afternoon, when Mr. Utterson found his way to Dr. Jekyll's door, where he was at once admitted by Poole, and carried down by the kitchen offices and across a yard which had once been a garden, to the building which was indifferently known as the laboratory or **dissecting** rooms. The doctor had bought the house from the **heirs** of a **celebrated** surgeon; and his own tastes being rather chemical than **anatomical**, had changed the [designation] of the block at the bottom of the garden. It was the first time that the lawyer had been received in that part of his friend's quarters; and he eyed the **dingy**, windowless structure with curiosity, and gazed round with a distasteful sense of strangeness as he crossed the theater, once crowded with eager students and now lying gaunt and silent, the tables **laden** with chemical **apparatus**, the floor **strewn** with crates and **littered** with packing straw, and the light falling dimly through the foggy **cupola**.

EXERCISE 1

SELF-TEST: After reading the above selection, do the following. Look at the Master Words below. Underline the words that you think you know. Circle the words that you are less sure about. Draw a square around the words you don't recognize.

MASTER WORDS	
anatomical	**dissect**
apparatus	**heir**
celebrated	**laden**
cupola	**litter**
dingy	**strewn**

EXERCISE 2

Read the selection on the preceding page again, this time paying special attention to the ten Master Words. In the (a) spaces provided below, write down what you think is the meaning of the word. After you have attempted a definition for each word, look up the word in a dictionary. In the (b) spaces, copy the appropriate dictionary definition.

1. **anatomical** (adj.)
   a. ____________________
   b. related to the scientific study of structure, either animal or plant

2. **apparatus** (n.)
   a. ____________________
   b. materials or machinery designed for a function

3. **celebrated** (adj.)
   a. ____________________
   b. distinguished or famous; occasionally, infamous

4. **cupola** (n.)
   a. ____________________
   b. a small structure, usually domed, built on a roof

5. **dingy** (adj.)
   a. ____________________
   b. grimy; smoky; soiled

6. **dissect** (v.)
   a. ____________________
   b. to divide into parts; to cut up; also, to analyze

7. **heir** (n.)
   a. ____________________
   b. successor of one who has died; one who inherits property

8. **laden** (adj.)
   a. ____________________
   b. burdened; loaded

9. **litter** (v.)
   a. ____________________
   b. to scatter rubbish and waste about

10. **strewn** (adj.)
    a. ____________________
    b. spread about; covered over

EXERCISE 3

Use the following list of synonyms and antonyms to fill in the blanks. Some words have no antonyms. In such cases, the antonym blanks have been marked with an X.

ancestor	descendant	instrument	physiological
basement	dome	loaded	sew up
beautify	empty	manual labor	spiritual
cleared	famous	obscure	sparkling
defile	grimy	open	tossed

	Synonyms	**Antonyms**
1. **dissect**	(open)	(sew up)
2. **heir**	(descendant)	(ancestor)
3. **celebrated**	(famous)	(obscure)
4. **anatomical**	(physiological)	(spiritual)
5. **dingy**	(grimy)	(sparkling)
6. **laden**	(loaded)	(empty)
7. **apparatus**	(instrument)	(manual labor)
8. **strewn**	(tossed)	(cleared)
9. **litter**	(defile)	(beautify)
10. **cupola**	(dome)	(basement)

EXERCISE 4

Decide whether the first pair in the items below are synonyms or antonyms. Then choose the Master Word that shows a similar relation to the word(s) preceding the blank.

1. discernment	:unawareness	::clean up	: (litter)
2. mute	:speechless	::bodily	: (anatomical)
3. impulse	:whim	::equipment	: (apparatus)
4. fatigue	:vitality	::unburdened	: (laden)
5. arbitrate	:argue	::unknown	: (celebrated)
6. contradictory	:supportive	::ancestor	: (heir)
7. instinct	:natural tendency	::steeple	: (cupola)
8. resolve	:iron will	::dismember	: (dissect)
9. capable	:unable	::shining	: (dingy)
10. straits	:predicament	::spread about	: (strewn)

EXERCISE 5

The Master Words in this lesson are repeated below. From the Master Words, choose the appropriate word for the blank in each of the following sentences. Write the word in the numbered space provided at the right.

anatomical	celebrated	dingy	heir	litter
apparatus	cupola	dissect	laden	strewn

1. At a cost of $2,000, Hawthorne had (a, an) ...?... erected on the roof of Wayside. 1. (cupola)
2. TV commercials chide viewers about their ...?... washes. 2. (dingy)
3. Our cookies are ...?... with large amounts of chocolate chips. 3. (laden)
4. Devoted naturalists will not ...?... the natural environment with any man-made products. 4. (litter)
5. Big, colorful ...?... charts told me immediately we must be in the biology class. 5. (anatomical)
6. Photography would be a lot more fun if you could carry less ...?... . 6. (apparatus)
7. The most ...?... frog in Calaveras County, California, was the one Mark Twain wrote about. 7. (celebrated)
8. Wreckage from the two-car crash was ...?... along the highway. 8. (strewn)
9. He appeared to be the only ...?... to the Amberson millions. 9. (heir)
10. Zoology students have mixed feelings about the project which calls for them to ...?... a frog. 10. (dissect)

EXERCISE 6

To complete the word spiral, choose the Master Word associated with each phrase below. Start with 1 and fill in each answer clockwise. Be careful! Each new word may overlap the previous word by one or more letters.

1. Victorian buildings usually had one
2. bogged down with packages
3. wherever there's a will, hopefully
4. world renowned
5. windows, if you don't wash them
6. skeletons, for example
7. to dispose of improperly
8. you might do this in biology class
9. a Bunsen burner, for example
10. describes clothes lying all over

1. C	U	P	O	2. L	A	D	E
6. A	N	A	T	O	M	I	N
Y	C	T	9. A	P	P	C	3. H
G	E	R	E	W	A	A	E
N	S	T	■	N	R	7. L	I
I	S	10. S	U	T	A	I	R
5. D	I	8. D	R	E	T	T	4. C
E	T	A	R	B	E	L	E

LESSON 21

Read the following selection to get the general meaning. Read it a second time, paying special attention to the words in dark type. Notice how they are used in sentences. These are Master Words. These are the words you will be working with in this section.

from ***Dear Future***
by Fred D'Aguiar

Gamediser heaved his right leg, then his left, then, using his fleshy fingers to grip the door frame, his entire bulk out of the country's only Pontiac. The car's suspension bounced him from a slope to its permanent lean towards the driver's side damaged by the **sustained** punishment of shouldering Gamediser. He stopped at Ariel ostensibly for a drink. Children and adults minding their stalls in the market square gathered to inspect the country's only Pontiac, allowed in against **stringent** import controls; without the slightest trace of **inhibition**, they stared at the body it had to convey, the heaviest person on the presidential payroll.

In confirmation of his grand-piano proportions Gamediser was also one of the President's least **dispensable** assets, second only to Brukup, with whom he shared the same height, five foot five inches, and a mutual dislike. Gamediser hated even to think about Brukup; it put him off his food. Since he was always about to eat or concluding a meal or in pursuit of a meal, virtually no room was left in his thoughts (on a conscious level) for Brukup. He hated Brukup's frugal nature: riding a bicycle when he should have been in something big, bright and imported. This **abstinence** presumably ran in the man's very **demeanour**: his thin legs, narrow bicycle, **sparse** vocabulary and needling eyes that pierced everything they hit, yet managed never to rest on anything for more than a moment. Gamediser knew that these very qualities made Brukup the President's right-hand man and **relegated** him to a permanent second place since he could never hope to emulate them. His eyes did not **alight** on things fleetingly, they landed squarely on them and consumed them. He did not speak in hushed tones, nor find the smallest number of words that would capture precisely what he wanted to say. Voluble and loud, he flavoured everything with **copious** amounts of description.

EXERCISE 1

SELF-TEST: After reading the above selection, do the following. Look at the Master Words below. Underline the words that you think you know. Circle the words that you are less sure about. Draw a square around the words you don't recognize.

MASTER WORDS

abstinence	**inhibition**
alight	**relegated**
copious	**sparse**
demeanour (demeanor)	**stringent**
dispensable	**sustained**

EXERCISE 2

Read the selection on the preceding page again, this time paying special attention to the ten Master Words. In the (a) spaces provided below, write down what you think is the meaning of the word. After you have attempted a definition for each word, look up the word in a dictionary. In the (b) spaces, copy the appropriate dictionary definition.

1. **abstinence** (n.)

   a. __________

   b. voluntarily refraining from partaking of an appetite or craving

2. **alight** (v.)

   a. __________

   b. come down from something

3. **copious** (adj.)

   a. __________

   b. full of thought, information, or matter

4. **demeanor** (n.)

   a. __________

   b. behavior toward others: outward manner

5. **dispensable** (adj.)

   a. __________

   b. capable of being or doing without

6. **inhibition** (n.)

   a. __________

   b. an inner impediment to free activity, expression, or functioning

7. **relegated** (v.)

   a. __________

   b. assigned to an appropriate place or situation on the basis of classification or appraisal

8. **sparse** (adj.)

   a. __________

   b. limited; not well-developed

9. **stringent** (adj.)

   a. __________

   b. marked by rigor, strictness, or severity especially with regard to rules or standards

10. **sustained** (adj.)

    a. __________

    b. prolonged; continual

EXERCISE 3

Use the following list of synonyms and antonyms to fill in the blanks. Some of the words have no antonyms. In such cases, the antonym blanks have been marked with an X.

abundant	indulgence	necessary	restraint	spontaneity
assigned	insufficient	plentiful	scanty	strict
behavior	land	prolonged	self-denial	unnecessary
brief	lenient			

	Synonyms	Antonyms
1. **sustained**	(prolonged)	(brief)
2. **stringent**	(strict)	(lenient)
3. **inhibition**	(self-denial or restraint)	(spontaneity or indulgence)
4. **dispensable**	(unnecessary)	(necessary)
5. **abstinence**	(restraint or self-denial)	(indulgence or spontaneity)
6. **demeanor**	(behavior)	X
7. **sparse**	(scanty)	(plentiful or abundant)
8. **relegated**	(assigned)	X
9. **alight**	(land)	X
10. **copious**	(abundant or plentiful)	(insufficient or scanty)

EXERCISE 4

Decide whether the first pair in the items below are synonyms or antonyms. Then choose the Master Word that shows a similar relation to the word(s) preceding the blank.

1. agenda	:plan	::strict	: (stringent)
2. raid	:invasion	::assigned	: (relegated)
3. refined	:gross	::necessary	: (dispensable)
4. illness	:malady	::abundant	: (copious)
5. encourage	:impede	::indulgence	: (abstinence)
6. wily	:clever	::restraint	: (inhibition)
7. amusement	:game	::behavior	: (demeanor)
8. envy	:jealousy	::land	: (alight)
9. adore	:detest	::plentiful	: (sparse)
10. require	:prohibit	::brief	: (sustained)

EXERCISE 5

The Master Words in this lesson are repeated below. From the Master Words, choose the appropriate word for the blank in each of the following sentences. Write the word in the numbered space provided at the right.

abstinence	copious	dispensable	relegated	stringent
alight	demeanor	inhibition	sparse	sustained

1. The rules at his new school seemed far more ...?... than at his old school. 1. (stringent)
2. Her fear of speaking before people arose from (a, an) ...?... she had had all her life. 2. (inhibition)
3. The colorful bird managed to ...?... under the eaves, out of the wind. 3. (alight)
4. They credited the improvement in their grades to ...?... effort. 4. (sustained)
5. Vegetation and rainfall were ...?... , causing little life to settle there. 5. (sparse)
6. In order to cope with difficulties in life, it helps to have a cheerful ...?... . 6. (demeanor)
7. When cutbacks had to be made at the factory, some of the workers realized they were ...?... . 7. (dispensable)
8. As part of their training, they practiced total ...?... from red meat. 8. (abstinence)
9. "In order to save any of the crops, we'll need ...?... amounts of rain," the farmer stated 9. (copious)
10. As a result of dropping the fly ball, he was ...?... to the bench for the rest of the game. 10. (relegated)

EXERCISE 6

This exercise compares groups of words according to their relative degree or intensity. Indicate their relative levels of degree or intensity by placing an L for lowest, an M for medium, or an H for highest in the appropriate blank. Master Words may be used in a different form. The first word or phrase in each series gives you the standard for comparison. See the example below.

how hot: __L__ warm __M__ sultry __H__ scorching

(*Warm* indicates the least heat, *sultry* a medium amount, and *scorching* the highest amount of heat.)

1. duration:	__M__ temporary	__L__ brief	__H__ sustained
2. importance:	__H__ vital	__L__ dispensable	__M__ useful
3. large amount:	__L__ sparse	__H__ copious	__M__ adequate
4. strictness:	__M__ firm	__H__ stringent	__L__ lenient
5. self-discipline:	__L__ indulgence	__M__ moderation	__H__ abstinence

LESSON 22

Read the following selection to get the general meaning. Read it a second time, paying special attention to the words in dark type. Notice how they are used in sentences. These are Master Words. These are the words you will be working with in this lesson.

From "**Peter Goldthwaite's Treasure**"
by Nathaniel Hawthorne

Never, in any of his **vagaries**, though each had made him happy while it lasted, had Peter been happier than now. Perhaps, after all, there was something in Peter Goldthwaite's turn of mind, which brought him an inward **recompense** for all the external evil that it caused. If he were poor, ill-clad, even hungry, and exposed, as it were, to be utterly annihilated by a **precipice** of **impending** ruin, yet only his body remained in these miserable circumstances, while his **aspiring** soul enjoyed the sunshine of a bright futurity. It was his nature to be always young, and the tendency of his mode of life to keep him so. Gray hairs were nothing, no, nor wrinkles, nor **infirmity**; he might look old, indeed, and be somewhat disagreeably connected with a **gaunt** old figure, much the worse for wear; but the true, the essential Peter was a young man of high hopes, just entering on the world. At the **kindling** of each new fire, his burnt-out youth rose afresh from the old embers and ashes. It rose **exulting** now. Having lived thus long—not too long, but just to the right age—a **susceptible** bachelor, with warm and tender dreams, he resolved, so long as the hidden gold should flash to light, to go a-wooing, and win the love of the fairest maid in town. What heart could resist him?

EXERCISE 1

SELF-TEST: After reading the above selection, do the following. Look at the Master Words below. Underline the words that you think you know. Circle the words that you are less sure about. Draw a square around the words you don't recognize.

MASTER WORDS

aspire	**kindling**
exult	**precipice**
gaunt	**recompense**
impending	**susceptible**
infirmity	**vagary**

EXERCISE 2

Read the selection on the preceding page again, this time paying special attention to the ten Master Words. In the (a) spaces provided below, write down what you think is the meaning of the word. After you have attempted a definition for each word, look up the word in a dictionary. In the (b) spaces, copy the appropriate dictionary definition.

1. **aspire** (v.)
   a. ______
   b. to seek a higher goal

2. **exult** (v.)
   a. ______
   b. to feel overjoyed; to be in high spirits

3. **gaunt** (adj.)
   a. ______
   b. thin and bony; lean

4. **impending** (adj.)
   a. ______
   b. soon to occur; approaching

5. **infirmity** (n.)
   a. ______
   b. feebleness; illness; weakness; shortcoming

6. **kindling** (v.)
   a. ______
   b. igniting; lighting

7. **precipice** (n.)
   a. ______
   b. face of a cliff; steep place

8. **recompense** (n.)
   a. ______
   b. payment; compensation

9. **susceptible** (adj.)
   a. ______
   b. especially sensitive; easily affected, as by disease

10. **vagary** (n.)
    a. ______
    b. odd or eccentric action

EXERCISE 3

Use the following list of synonyms and antonyms to fill in the blanks. Some words have no antonyms. In such cases, the antonym blanks have been marked with an X.

caprice	igniting	payment	strive
cliff	indebtedness	plateau	suffocating
grieve	imminent	predisposed	unlikely
haggard	immune	rejoice	vigor
healthy	loaf	stability	weakness

	Synonyms	Antonyms
1. **vagary**	(caprice)	(stability)
2. **recompense**	(payment)	(indebtedness)
3. **precipice**	(cliff)	(plateau)
4. **impending**	(imminent)	(unlikely)
5. **aspire**	(strive)	(loaf)
6. **gaunt**	(haggard)	(healthy)
7. **infirmity**	(weakness)	(vigor)
8. **kindling**	(igniting)	(suffocating)
9. **exult**	(rejoice)	(grieve)
10. **susceptible**	(predisposed)	(immune)

EXERCISE 4

Decide whether the first pair in the items below are synonyms or antonyms. Then choose the Master Word that shows a similar relation to the word(s) preceding the blank.

1. lofty	:lowly	::plump	: (gaunt)
2. solemn	:lighthearted	::invulnerable	: (susceptible)
3. oppressive	:reviving	::strength	: (infirmity)
4. vellum	:parchment	::attempt	: (aspire)
5. tread	:trampling	::whim	: (vagary)
6. foreboding	:optimism	::suffer	: (exult)
7. luxurious	:simple	::lowland	: (precipice)
8. livery	:uniform	::lighting	: (kindling)
9. theology	:doctrine	::approaching	: (impending)
10. natty	:dressy	::reward	: (recompense)

EXERCISE 5

The Master Words in this lesson are repeated below. From the Master Words, choose the appropriate word for the blank in each of the following sentences. Write the word in the numbered space provided at the right.

aspire	gaunt	infirmity	precipice	susceptible
exult	impending	kindling	recompense	vagary

1. Despite his ...?..., Kowalski played, and his slight limp was noticed. 1. (infirmity)
2. The recognition of athletes is small ...?... for the service they provide school and community. 2. (recompense)
3. Knute Rockne's pep talks were capable of ...?... great hope in the hearts of Notre Dame players. 3. (kindling)
4. After combat, Ted seemed more ...?... to nervous shock. 4. (susceptible)
5. Another conference championship and an Orange Bowl bid gave the crowd good cause to ...?... . 5. (exult)
6. Some models starve themselves to appear ...?... . 6. (gaunt)
7. The whole family recognized Grandpa's insistence that "we were just a passel of Yankee blockheads" as just another passing ...?... . 7. (vagary)
8. Looking over the ...?..., she saw the river winding through the valley below. 8. (precipice)
9. Good speech and manners and a way with people are important if you ...?... to political office. 9. (aspire)
10. Bright boils of lightening told the seriousness of the ...?... storm. 10. (impending)

EXERCISE 6

Write the Master Word that is associated with each word group below. Then list three things that might be associated with the review word that follows.

1. fuse, fire, passion (kindling)
2. prisoners of war, hunger, skeletal (gaunt)
3. colds, flattery, scams (susceptible)
4. paycheck, award, verdict (recompense)
5. yuppies, ambition, ideal (aspire)
6. diving, lover's leap, mountain climbing (precipice)
7. hurrah, championship, jump for joy (exult)
8. Alzheimer's disease, wheelchair, old age (infirmity)
9. future, deadline, death (impending)
10. weather, wanderers, eccentrics (vagary)

Review word: dispensable (Lesson 21)

(tissue) (garbage) (fat)

(Note: Answers may vary.)

LESSON 23

Read the following selection to get the general meaning. Read it a second time, paying special attention to the words in dark type. Notice how they are used in sentences. These are Master Words. These are the words you will be working with in this lesson.

From "**Omphale: A Rococo Story**"
by Theophile Gauthier

The moon shone full upon the window-panes, and projected her **wan** bluish light into the room. Vast shadows, fantastic forms, were **defined** upon the floor and the walls. The clock chimed a quarter, and the **vibration** of the sound took a long time to die away: it seemed like a sigh. The plainly **audible** strokes of the pendulum seemed like the **pulsations** of a young heart, throbbing with passion.

I felt anything but comfortable; and a very **bewilderment** of fear took possession of me.

A furious gust of wind banged the shutters and made the window-sashes tremble. The woodwork cracked; the tapestry **undulated**. I ventured to glance in the direction of Omphale, with a vague suspicion that she was instrumental in all this unpleasantness, for some secret purpose of her own. I was not mistaken.

The tapestry became violently agitated. Omphale **detached** herself from the wall and leaped lightly to the carpet: she came straight towards my bed, after having first turned herself carefully in my direction. I fancy it will hardly be necessary to describe my **stupefaction**. The most **intrepid** old soldier would not have felt very comfortable under similar circumstances; and I was neither old nor a soldier. I awaited the end of the adventure in terrified silence.

EXERCISE 1

SELF-TEST: After reading the above selection, do the following. Look at the Master Words below. Underline the words that you think you know. Circle the words that you are less sure about. Draw a square around the words you don't recognize.

MASTER WORDS	
audible	**pulsation**
bewilderment	**stupefaction**
define	**undulate**
detach	**vibration**
intrepid	**wan**

EXERCISE 2

Read the selection on the preceding page again, this time paying special attention to the ten Master Words. In the (a) spaces provided below, write down what you think is the meaning of the word. After you have attempted a definition for each word, look up the word in a dictionary. In the (b) spaces, copy the appropriate dictionary definition.

1. **audible** (adj.)
   a. ______
   b. capable of being heard; detectable by ear

2. **bewilderment** (n.)
   a. ______
   b. state of confusion or disorientation

3. **define** (v.)
   a. ______
   b. to outline; to explain or describe; to distinguish

4. **detach** (v.)
   a. ______
   b. to separate from; to remove

5. **intrepid** (adj.)
   a. ______
   b. courageous; brave; fearless

6. **pulsation** (n.)
   a. ______
   b. rhythmic throbbing; vibration

7. **stupefaction** (n.)
   a. ______
   b. astonishment; amazement

8. **undulate** (v.)
   a. ______
   b. to move in a heaving fashion, as in the manner of waves

9. **vibration** (n.)
   a. ______
   b. trembling motion

10. **wan** (adj.)
    a. ______
    b. pale or sickly; pallid

EXERCISE 3

Use the following list of synonyms and antonyms to fill in the blanks. Some words have no antonyms. In such cases, the antonym blanks have been marked with an X.

amazement	calm	craven	pale
arrhythmia	certainty	disconnect	puzzlement
aural	colorful	hushed	shimmy
billow	confuse	interpret	smoothness
boredom	courageous	join	throbbing

	Synonyms	Antonyms
1. **vibration**	(shimmy)	(smoothness)
2. **wan**	(pale)	(colorful)
3. **define**	(interpret)	(confuse)
4. **audible**	(aural)	(hushed)
5. **pulsation**	(throbbing)	(arrhythmia)
6. **bewilderment**	(puzzlement)	(certainty)
7. **undulate**	(billow)	(calm)
8. **detach**	(disconnect)	(join)
9. **stupefaction**	(amazement)	(boredom)
10. **intrepid**	(courageous)	(craven)

EXERCISE 4

Decide whether the first pair in the items below are synonyms or antonyms. Then choose the Master Word that shows a similar relation to the word(s) preceding the blank.

1. recompense	:amends	::beating	: (vibration)(pulsation)
2. vagary	:impulse	::ripple	: (undulate)
3. aspire	:despair	::obscure	: (define)
4. impending	:distant	::cowardly	: (intrepid)
5. precipice	:bluff	::confusion	: (bewilderment)
6. gaunt	:thin	::trembling	: (pulsation)(vibration)
7. infirmity	:vitality	::disinterest	: (stupefaction)
8. kindling	:burning	::unfasten	: (detach)
9. exult	:mourn	::noiseless	: (audible)
10. susceptible	:defenseless	::pallid	: (wan)

EXERCISE 5

The Master Words in this lesson are repeated below. From the Master Words, choose the appropriate word for the blank in each of the following sentences. Write the word in the numbered space provided at the right.

audible	define	intrepid	stupefaction	vibration
bewilderment	detach	pulsation	undulate	wan

1. During her illness, Mary became ...?... and listless. 1. (wan)
2. The artist's rough lines helped ...?... the figure of a man under a city streetlight. 2. (define)
3. In the elegant ballroom, the great hoop skirts would ...?... as the dancers glided across the polished floor. 3. (undulate)
4. From the back of the room, the speaker's voice was barely ...?... . 4. (audible)
5. The wide eyes and open mouth indicated the child's ...?... when he saw his first giraffe. 5. (stupefaction)
6. To get credit for payment, be sure to ...?... this stub and mail it with your check. 6. (detach)
7. Most of Roger's ...?... resulted from his taking solid geometry and calculus at the same time—enough to throw anybody. 7. (bewilderment)
8. The ...?... Odysseus had fought heroically in the Trojan War. 8. (intrepid)
9. The doctor could detect no ...?... of the man's heart following the attack. 9. (pulsation)
10. The earthquake was so mild that most people were only aware of a slight ...?... . 10. (vibration)

EXERCISE 6

Use at least five Master Words from this lesson to write a scene about one of the following topics. Or create a topic of your own. Write your choice on the blank. Circle the Master Words as you use them.

Possible Topics: Ski Adventure, High-wire Act

(Note: Answers will vary.)

LESSON 24

Part I: From the list below, choose the correct word for each sentence that follows. Use each word only once.

anecdote	discernment	impending	procedure
apparatus	dismal	perpetual	stupefaction
dearth	fragile	precarious	verge

1. The drama critic was known for his great powers of ___(discernment)___ in choosing the best new plays.
2. Balanced in (a, an) ___(precarious)___ position on the cliff, John stared fearfully down into the deep, jagged ravine.
3. If you follow the same ___(procedure)___ in each case, you will be able to finish quickly.
4. A mood of ___(impending)___ defeat filled the locker room at halftime.
5. The quack doctor assembled his curious-looking ___(apparatus)___ in order to impress his gullible patient.
6. He stood there with his mouth open in a state of complete ___(stupefaction)___ over his wife's strange behavior.
7. Who would have thought that such a large tree could be so ___(fragile)___ in the face of a tornado?
8. The acreage, described in glowing words in the advertisement, actually lay in (a, an) ___(dismal)___ swamp.
9. Janet, the most nervous person I've ever known, was in (a, an) ___(perpetual)___ state of worry.
10. The teacher often used a personal ___(anecdote)___ about her experience in London to end the English class.
11. She was on the ___(verge)___ of confessing to the crime when another suspect was arrested.
12. (A, An) ___(dearth)___ of jobs in the state led many people to emigrate.

Part II: From the list below, choose the correct word for each sentence that follows. Use each word only once.

arbitrate	dispensable	grandeur	stealthily
crevice	exult	headlong	sustained
dilapidation	fatigue	jovial	version

1. Surrounded by the ___(grandeur)___ of the Roman ruins, all we could do was stare in awe.
2. Some people exercise to the point of ___(fatigue)___.
3. The victim's story didn't match the ___(version)___ told by the eyewitness.
4. Because of a lack of care, the old mansion had fallen into a state of ___(dilapidation)___.
5. The candidate's supporters ___(exult)___ (d, ed) over her stunning upset victory.

6. He was daydreaming about Samantha, which is why he and his bike crashed ______(headlong)______ into the garbage cans.

7. Anne's foot became lodged in (a, an) ______(crevice)______ as she attempted to climb the mountain.

8. Mr. Robbins was actually quite ______(jovial)______—just the opposite of what his scowling picture had led us to expect.

9. The stairs were worn on the edges, especially in the middle, having ______(sustained)______ so much traffic over the years.

10. Our backpacks were crammed full so we had to decide what was ______(dispensable)______ and what wasn't.

11. Slowly and ______(stealthily)______, the lion crept through the long grass toward the straggler from the antelope herd.

12. Since we could not resolve the dispute ourselves, we agreed to ask the director to ______(arbitrate)______ the matter for us.

Part III: Decide whether the first pair in the items below are synonyms or antonyms. Then choose a Master Word from Lessons 13–23 that shows a similar relation to the word(s) preceding the blank. Do not repeat a Master Word that appears in the first column.

1. relieve	:deliver	::high-pitched	:	(shrill)
2. gratify	:please	::weakness	:	(infirmity)
3. economical	:unthrifty	::enlightenment	:	(bewilderment)
4. capable	:qualified	::reimbursement	:	(recompense)
5. laden	:unfilled	::feeling	:	(numbness)
6. picturesque	:charming	::strict	:	(stringent)
7. demeanor	:style	::determination	:	(resolve)
8. limpid	:cloudy	::pallid	:	(ruddy)
9. flawed	:blemished	::urge	:	(impulse)
10. fragile	:tender	::dream	:	(aspire)
11. whoop	:shout	::character	:	(demeanour)
12. harmonic	:dissonant	::expectantly	:	(despairingly)
13. sly	:open	::indulgence	:	(abstinence)
14. intrepid	:afraid	::necessary	:	(dispensable)
15. defiance	:submission	::unite	:	(detach)
16. indifferent	:concerned	::delight	:	(pique)
17. infinite	:endless	::colorless	:	(wan)
18. strive	:work	::insensitive	:	(unconscious)
19. celebrated	:unnoticed	::normalcy	:	(vagary)

LESSON 25

Read the following selection to get the general meaning. Read it a second time, paying special attention to the words in dark type. Notice how they are used in sentences. These are Master Words. These are the words you will be working with in this lesson.

From "**Tennessee's Partner**"
by Bret Harte

Meanwhile a popular feeling against Tennessee had grown up on the Bar. He was known to be a gambler; he was suspected to be a thief. In these suspicions Tennessee's Partner was equally suspect; his continued **intimacy** with Tennessee after the affair above quoted could only be accounted for on the **hypothesis** of a co-partnership of crime. At last Tennessee's guilt became **flagrant.** One day he overtook a stranger on his way to Red Dog. The stranger afterward **related** that Tennessee **beguiled** the time with interesting anecdote and **reminiscence**, but illogically concluded the interview in the following words: "And now, young man, I'll trouble you for your knife, your pistols, and your money. You see your weppings might get you into trouble at Red Dog, and your money's a temptation to the evilly disposed. I think you said your address was San Francisco. I shall **endeavor** to call." It may be stated here that Tennessee had a fine flow of humor, which no business **preoccupation** could wholly **subdue**.

The exploit was his last. Red Dog and Sandy Bar made common cause against the highwayman. Tennessee was hunted in very much the same fashion as his **prototype**, the grizzly. As the web closed around him, he made a desperate dash through the Bar. . . .

EXERCISE 1

SELF-TEST: After reading the above selection, do the following. Look at the Master Words below. Underline the words that you think you know. Circle the words that you are less sure about. Draw a square around the words you don't recognize.

MASTER WORDS	
beguile	**preoccupation**
endeavor	**prototype**
flagrant	**relate**
hypothesis	**reminiscence**
intimacy	**subdue**

EXERCISE 2

Read the selection on the preceding page again, this time paying special attention to the ten Master Words. In the (a) spaces provided below, write down what you think is the meaning of the word. After you have attempted a definition for each word, look up the word in a dictionary. In the (b) spaces, copy the appropriate dictionary definition.

1. **beguile** (v.)
   a. ______
   b. to pass; to while away; to spend
2. **endeavor** (v.)
   a. ______
   b. to strive; to attempt; to try
3. **flagrant** (adj.)
   a. ______
   b. conspicuous; obvious; undisguised; deliberate
4. **hypothesis** (n.)
   a. ______
   b. possible solution; tentative theory or explanation
5. **intimacy** (n.)
   a. ______
   b. closeness; familiarity
6. **preoccupation** (n.)
   a. ______
   b. state of being engrossed; concern; diversion; distraction of thought
7. **prototype** (n.)
   a. ______
   b. pattern or model
8. **relate** (v.)
   a. ______
   b. to narrate; to tell; to recount
9. **reminiscence** (n.)
   a. ______
   b. the act of recalling things, people, and events
10. **subdue** (v.)
    a. ______
    b. to crush; to vanquish; to control by force

EXERCISE 3

Use the following list of synonyms and antonyms to fill in the blanks. Some words have no antonyms. In such cases, the antonym blanks have been marked with an X.

absorption	familiarity	prescience	spend
alertness	furtive	recollection	tell
attempt	glaring	remoteness	theory
derivation	liberate	restrain	vegetate
fact	mock-up		

	Synonyms	Antonyms
1. **prototype**	(mock-up)	(derivation)
2. **intimacy**	(familiarity)	(remoteness)
3. **hypothesis**	(theory)	(fact)
4. **flagrant**	(glaring)	(furtive)
5. **relate**	(tell)	X
6. **beguile**	(spend)	X
7. **reminiscence**	(recollection)	(prescience)
8. **endeavor**	(attempt)	(vegetate)
9. **preoccupation**	(absorption)	(alertness)
10. **subdue**	(restrain)	(liberate)

EXERCISE 4

Decide whether the first pair in the items below are synonyms or antonyms. Then choose the Master Word that shows a similar relation to the word(s) preceding the blank.

1. undulate	:wave	::explanation	: (hypothesis)
2. define	:describe	::pass	: (beguile)
3. wan	:ruddy	::release	: (subdue)
4. vibration	:shaking	::try	: (endeavor)
5. stupefaction	:astonishment	::memory	: (reminiscence)
6. pulsation	:beating	::obvious	: (flagrant)
7. audible	:unheard	::distance	: (intimacy)
8. bewilderment	:understanding	::attention	: (preoccupation)
9. detach	:connect	::copy	: (prototype)
10. intrepid	:fearful	::withhold	: (relate)

EXERCISE 5

The Master Words in this lesson are repeated below. From the Master Words, choose the appropriate word for the blank in each of the following sentences. Write the word in the numbered space provided at the right.

beguile	flagrant	intimacy	prototype	reminiscence
endeavor	hypothesis	preoccupation	relate	subdue

1. There is often ...?... about old times at family reunions. 1. (reminiscence)
2. The police and National Guard were able to ...?... the rioters. 2. (subdue)
3. This is merely (a, an) ...?... of the new monorail proposed for selected cities. 3. (prototype)
4. ...?... moves from theory to law after it has been tested by scientific methods. 4. (Hypothesis)
5. Cameras search the faces of characters to give modern films a close-up ...?... . 5. (intimacy)
6. Mario planned to ...?... the time away by snoozing in a hammock. 6. (beguile)
7. The wing man was awarded two free shots after the ...?... foul by the opposing guard. 7. (flagrant)
8. ...?... with personal matters kept him from attending to even the most brilliant lecture. 8. (Preoccupation)
9. After the arrest, he had to ...?... the unusual hold-up story to police. 9. (relate)
10. We will ...?... to correct any problems that have been caused by our management. 10. (endeavor)

EXERCISE 6

Order the words in each item from *least* to *most.* Use the abbreviations *L* for "least" and *M* for "most." Leave the line before the word of the middle degree blank. The first word provides a clue about how to arrange the words. See the example.

exact: M proportions ____estimation L guess
(*Guess* indicates the least exact; *proportions* indicates the most exact.)

1. warmth:	(M) intimacy	____friendliness	(L) indifference
2. forceful:	____order	(L) caution	(M) subdue
3. effort:	____endeavor	(M) overexert	(L) loaf
4. definite:	____hypothesis	(L) guess	(M) proof
5. intentional:	(M) flagrant	(L) accidental	____planned
6. final:	____prototype	(M) end product	(L) idea
7. known:	____hint	(L) hush up	(M) relate
8. productive:	____work	(L) beguile	(M) accomplish
9. conscious:	(L) dream	(M) experience	____reminiscence
10. attentive:	____preoccupation	(L) unconsciousness	(M) concentration

(Note: In some cases, answers may vary.)

LESSON 26

Read the following selection to get the general meaning. Read it a second time, paying special attention to the words in dark type. Notice how they are used in sentences. These are Master Words. These are the words you will be working with in this section.

from ***Falling Leaves: The True Story of an Unwanted Chinese Daughter***
by Adeline Yen Mah

Our tour group flew into Beijing on New Year's Eve, arriving on a sunny but cold afternoon. On the roof of the new airport **terminal**, a giant photograph of Chairman Mao **beamed** down, **flanked** by two huge scarlet Chinese characters, 北京 Beijing (Northern Capital). Through loudspeakers came the **lilting** Mandarin of a female announcer, "Beijing welcomes you!"

As we emerged from an immigration booth, a small, **stocky** middle-aged Chinese woman rushed towards us. Her black hair was badly dyed and she wore a brown coat with a fake fur collar. *"Wu mei!"* she called. "五妹 *Wu mei* (Fifth Younger Sister)*!* Is that you?"

No one had called me *wu mei* since those **forlorn** days of my Shanghai childhood. She was now standing in front of me, smiling from ear to ear. Something about her **posture**, the shoulders a little **lopsided** and uneven, the roundish flat face **tilted**, the semi-paralysed left hand held tightly by her right with all ten fingers **interlaced**, struck a chord from long ago. Involuntarily my tongue twisted into the familiar Chinese language of early childhood. "姊姊 *Jie jie* (Elder Sister)," I answered respectfully. "It is I."

EXERCISE 1

SELF-TEST: After reading the above selection, do the following. Look at the Master Words below. Underline the words that you think you know. Circle the words that you are less sure about. Draw a square around the words you don't recognize.

MASTER WORDS	
beamed	**lopsided**
flanked	**posture**
forlorn	**stocky**
interlaced	**terminal**
lilting	**tilted**

EXERCISE 2

Read the selection on the preceding page again, this time paying special attention to the ten Master Words. In the (a) spaces provided below, write down what you think is the meaning of the word. After you have attempted a definition for each word, look up the word in a dictionary. In the (b) spaces, copy the appropriate dictionary definition.

1. **beamed** (v.)
   a. ______________________
   b. smiled with joy
2. **flanked** (adj.)
   a. ______________________
   b. situated at the side of or on both sides of
3. **forlorn** (adj.)
   a. ______________________
   b. sad and lonely because of isolation or desertion
4. **interlaced** (adj.)
   a. ______________________
   b. crossed as if woven together
5. **lilting** (adj.)
   a. ______________________
   b. rhythmically and with fluctuating pitch
6. **lopsided** (adj.)
   a. ______________________
   b. lacking in balance, symmetry, or proportion; disproportionately heavy on one side
7. **posture** (n.)
   a. ______________________
   b. the position or bearing of the body
8. **stocky** (adj.)
   a. ______________________
   b. compact, sturdy, and relatively thick in build)
9. **terminal** (n.)
   a. ______________________
   b. a passenger station that is central to a considerable area
10. **tilted** (adj.)
    a. ______________________
    b. moved or shifted so as to lean or incline

EXERCISE 3

Use the following list of synonyms and antonyms to fill in the blanks. Some of the words have no antonyms. In such cases, the antonym blanks have been marked with an X.

cheerful	grinned	scowled	stance	surrounded
crooked	interwoven	separated	station	unaccompanied
doleful	lively	slanted	straight	
even	monotonous	slight		

	Synonyms	Antonyms
1. **terminal**	(station)	X
2. **beamed**	(grinned)	(scowled)
3. **flanked**	(surrounded)	(unaccompanied)
4. **lilting**	(lively)	(monotonous)
5. **stocky**	(thickset)	(slight)
6. **forlorn**	(doleful)	(cheerful)
7. **posture**	(stance)	X
8. **lopsided**	(crooked or slanted)	(even or straight)
9. **tilted**	(slanted)	(straight)
10. **interlaced**	(interwoven)	(separated)

EXERCISE 4

Decide whether the first pair in the items below are synonyms or antonyms. Then choose the Master Word that shows a similar relation to the word(s) preceding the blank.

1. gentle	:brutal	::scowled	: (beamed)
2. anonymous	:unidentified	::station	: (terminal)
3. specific	:vague	::happy	: (forlorn)
4. uncanny	:unnatural	::slanted	: (tilted or lopsided)
5. absurd	:ridiculous	::bearing	: (posture)
6. flagrant	:furtive	::unaccompanied	: (flanked)
7. strenuous	:arduous	::interwoven	: (interlaced)
8. skill	:deftness	::expressive	: (lilting)
9. starving	:replete	::skinny	: (stocky)
10. sagging	:taut	::even	: (lopsided or tilted)

EXERCISE 5

The Master Words in this lesson are repeated below. From the Master Words, choose the appropriate word for the blank in each of the following sentences. Write the word in the numbered space provided at the right.

beamed	forlorn	lilting	posture	terminal
flanked	interlaced	lopsided	stocky	tilted

1. She sat on the train, looking out the window, with her fingers ...?... in her lap. — 1. (interlaced)
2. Because one shoulder was higher than the other, she presented (a, an) ...?... look when walking towards you. — 2. (lopsided or tilted)
3. The driveway to the mansion was ...?... with perfectly spaced white pine trees. — 3. (flanked)
4. Grandma's face ...?... as they approached, and she opened her arms to take them all in. — 4. (beamed)
5. He was as short and ...?... as she was tall and lanky. — 5. (stocky)
6. With his head hanging and shoulders drooping, Jeremy's ...?... spoke eloquently of his dejection. — 6. (posture)
7. Her melodious, ...?... voice on the radio helped wake them up each morning. — 7. (lilting)
8. She hurried to the ...?... to meet her guest, but the plane had already arrived. — 8. (terminal)
9. The display, which the children had worked on so hard, now looked dangerously ...?... to one side. — 9. (tilted or lopsided)
10. After the family left, she always felt a little ...?... . — 10. (forlorn)

EXERCISE 6

Complete the wordsearch puzzle.

beamed
flanked
forlorn
interlaced
lilting
lopsided
posture
stocky
terminal
tilted

D E C A L R E T N I N Y A X X
V Z A Q D O T D E K N A L F O
T P R G W E P I R R R Y U F H
J N Y E R U T S O P M Y N P G
A Z D K M N X L I L T I N G J
Q C Q J C Z R H I D Q Q N R K
O I T O W O V A E T E M U A L
L A S S F Y T M Z G Q D P M L
J P Z L B U A S F F K Z F Z O
D K L J U E M E Z U O Y W E F
T E I P B V R Y K U A L V B M

LESSON 27

Read the following selection to get the general meaning. Read it a second time, paying special attention to the words in dark type. Notice how they are used in sentences. These are Master Words. These are the words you will be working with in this lesson.

From "**Over on the T'other Mounting**"
by Mary Noailles Murfree

Stretching out **laterally** from a long **oblique** line of the Southern Alleghenies are two parallel ranges, following the same course through several leagues, and separated by a narrow strip of valley hardly half a mile in width. As they fare along arm in arm, so to speak, **sundry** differences between the close companions are distinctly **apparent**. One is much the higher, and leads the way; it strikes out all the bold curves and angles of the course, **meekly** attended by the lesser ridge; its shadowy coves and sharp ravines are repeated in miniature as its comrade falls into the line of march; it seems to have its companion in charge, and to conduct it away from the majestic procession of mountains that traverses the State.

But despite its more **imposing** appearance, all the **tangible** advantages are possessed by its humble neighbor. When Old Rocky-Top, as the lower range is called, is fresh and green with the tender **verdure** of spring, the snow still lies on the summit of the T'other Mounting, and drifts deep into **treacherous** rifts and chasms, and **muffles** the voice of the singing pines. . . .

EXERCISE 1

SELF-TEST: After reading the above selection, do the following. Look at the Master Words below. Underline the words that you think you know. Circle the words that you are less sure about. Draw a square around the words you don't recognize.

MASTER WORDS	
apparent	**oblique**
imposing	**sundry**
laterally	**tangible**
meek	**treacherous**
muffle	**verdure**

EXERCISE 2

Read the selection on the preceding page again, this time paying special attention to the ten Master Words. In the (a) spaces provided below, write down what you think is the meaning of the word. After you have attempted a definition for each word, look up the word in a dictionary. In the (b) spaces, copy the appropriate dictionary definition.

1. **apparent** (adj.)
   a. __________
   b. obvious; open to view; clearly seen
2. **imposing** (adj.)
   a. __________
   b. grand; overpowering; impressive
3. **laterally** (adv.)
   a. __________
   b. sideways; sidelong; across
4. **meek** (adj.)
   a. __________
   b. quiet; shy; unassuming; humble
5. **muffle** (v.)
   a. __________
   b. to subdue, usually as sound; also, to cover, conceal, or protect
6. **oblique** (adj.)
   a. __________
   b. slanting; not square or straight; indirect
7. **sundry** (adj.)
   a. __________
   b. varied; of many kinds; diverse
8. **tangible** (adj.)
   a. __________
   b. touchable; evident; having substance; real
9. **treacherous** (adj.)
   a. __________
   b. not trustworthy; sneaky; capable of villainy
10. **verdure** (n.)
    a. __________
    b. greenness, especially a garden, grass, or other luxurious vegetation

EXERCISE 3

Use the following list of synonyms and antonyms to fill in the blanks. Some words have no antonyms. In such cases, the antonym blanks have been marked with an X.

amplify	desert	obvious	similar
brash	direct	pasture	slanting
concealed	forward	shy	tenuous
concrete	impressive	sideways	trustworthy
deceitful	insignificant	silence	various

	Synonyms	Antonyms
1. **laterally**	(sideways)	(forward)
2. **oblique**	(slanting)	(direct)
3. **sundry**	(various)	(similar)
4. **apparent**	(obvious)	(concealed)
5. **meek**	(shy)	(brash)
6. **imposing**	(impressive)	(insignificant)
7. **tangible**	(concrete)	(tenuous)
8. **verdure**	(pasture)	(desert)
9. **treacherous**	(deceitful)	(trustworthy)
10. **muffle**	(silence)	(amplify)

EXERCISE 4

Decide whether the first pair in the items below are synonyms or antonyms. Then choose the Master Word that shows a similar relation to the word(s) preceding the blank.

1. prevail	:surrender	::straight	: (oblique)
2. exalt	:ridicule	::bold	: (meek)
3. bear	:shoulder	::crosswise	: (laterally)
4. harass	:torment	::vegetation	: (verdure)
5. ostentatious	:simple	::increase	: (muffle)
6. sulk	:cheer	::alike	: (sundry)
7. malice	:resentment	::grand	: (imposing)
8. chagrin	:annoyance	::real	: (tangible)
9. dejection	:hopefulness	::hidden	: (apparent)
10. flare	:burn	::unreliable	: (treacherous)

EXERCISE 5

The Master Words in this lesson are repeated below. From the Master Words, choose the appropriate word for the blank in each of the following sentences. Write the word in the numbered space provided at the right.

apparent	laterally	muffle	sundry	treacherous
imposing	meek	oblique	tangible	verdure

1. The forty-eight story insurance building in our town is one of the most ...?... edifices I know. — 1. (imposing)
2. The new tail pipe assembly unit failed to ...?... the engine sound enough to suit police. — 2. (muffle)
3. Ice covered highways across the state, making driving ...?... . — 3. (treacherous)
4. Some neighborhoods have (a, an) ...?... store which has almost as many good things as a supermarket. — 4. (sundry)
5. In football, a man in motion must move ...?... or backward from the scrimmage line. — 5. (laterally)
6. Humility is a virtue because the Bible promises that "the ...?... shall inherit the earth." — 6. (meek)
7. There was no ...?... damage to the car, but an expert could tell there was something wrong with the frame. — 7. (apparent)
8. The ...?... of the countryside makes spring the freshest season. — 8. (verdure)
9. The cash register gives you ...?... evidence of your day's effort. — 9. (tangible)
10. The ...?... rays of sunlight filtered through the window. — 10. (oblique)

EXERCISE 6

Use at least five Master Words from this lesson to write a scene about one of the following topics. Or create a topic of your own. Write your choice on the blank. Circle the Master Words as you use them.

Possible Topics: Winning Field Goal, Spy Games

(Note: Answers will vary.)

LESSON 28

Read the following selection to get the general meaning. Read it a second time, paying special attention to the words in dark type. Notice how they are used in sentences. These are Master Words. These are the words you will be working with in this lesson.

From "**The Man That Corrupted Hadleyburg**" by Mark Twain

It was many years ago, Hadleyburg was the most honest and upright town in all the region around about. It had kept that reputation **unsmirched** during three generations, and was prouder of it than of any other of its possessions. It was so proud of it, and so **anxious** to insure its **perpetuation**, that it began to teach the principles of honest dealing to its babies in the cradle, and made the like teachings the **staple** of their culture thenceforward through all the years devoted to their education. Also, throughout the **formative** years temptations were kept out of the way of the young people, so that their honesty could have every chance to harden and **solidify**, and become a part of their very bone. The neighboring towns were jealous of this honorable **supremacy**, and affected to **sneer** at Hadleyburg's pride in it and call it **vanity**; but all the same they were obliged to acknowledge that Hadleyburg was in reality an **incorruptible** town; and if pressed they would also acknowledge that the mere fact that a young man hailed from Hadleyburg was all the recommendation he needed when he went forth from his natal town to seek for responsible employment.

EXERCISE 1

SELF-TEST: After reading the above selection, do the following. Look at the Master Words below. Underline the words that you think you know. Circle the words that you are less sure about. Draw a square around the words you don't recognize.

MASTER WORDS

anxious	**solidify**
formative	**staple**
incorruptible	**supremacy**
perpetuation	**unsmirched**
sneer	**vanity**

EXERCISE 2

Read the selection on the preceding page again, this time paying special attention to the ten Master Words. In the (a) spaces provided below, write down what you think is the meaning of the word. After you have attempted a definition for each word, look up the word in a dictionary. In the (b) spaces, copy the appropriate dictionary definition.

1. **anxious** (adj.)
   a. ______
   b. concerned; worried; fretful
2. **formative** (adj.)
   a. ______
   b. capable of being shaped
3. **incorruptible** (adj.)
   a. ______
   b. pure and incapable of being corrupted or made sinful
4. **perpetuation** (n.)
   a. ______
   b. continuance; maintenance; lack of interruption
5. **sneer** (v.)
   a. ______
   b. to jeer, scoff, or scorn, sometimes with laughter, smiles, or facial expressions of contempt
6. **solidify** (v.)
   a. ______
   b. to become solid or compact; to change from liquid to solid state
7. **staple** (n.)
   a. ______
   b. a principal commodity; also, that which is most important and necessary
8. **supremacy** (n.)
   a. ______
   b. position of power or superiority
9. **unsmirched** (adj.)
   a. ______
   b. clean; unblemished; untarnished
10. **vanity** (n.)
    a. ______
    b. conceit; excess of pride; self-love

EXERCISE 3

Use the following list of synonyms and antonyms to fill in the blanks. Some words have no antonyms. In such cases, the antonym blanks have been marked with an X.

cessation	enslavement	indifferent	predominance
coagulate	fraudulent	liquify	pure
conceit	frill	modifying	spotless
concerned	gibe	necessity	tarnished
continuance	humility	praise	unalterable

	Synonyms	Antonyms
1. **unsmirched**	(spotless) (pure)	(tarnished) (fraudulent)
2. **anxious**	(concerned)	(indifferent)
3. **perpetuation**	(continuance)	(cessation)
4. **staple**	(necessity)	(frill)
5. **formative**	(modifying)	(unalterable)
6. **solidify**	(coagulate)	(liquify)
7. **supremacy**	(predominance)	(enslavement)
8. **sneer**	(gibe)	(praise)
9. **vanity**	(conceit)	(humility)
10. **incorruptible**	(pure) (spotless)	(fraudulent) (tarnished)

EXERCISE 4

Decide whether the first pair in the items below are synonyms or antonyms. Then choose the Master Word that shows a similar relation to the word(s) preceding the blank.

1. muffle	:magnify	::suspension	: (perpetuation)
2. imposing	:overpowering	::shapable	: (formative)
3. sundry	:uniform	::modesty	: (vanity)
4. laterally	:sideways	::jeer	: (sneer)
5. treacherous	:disloyal	::harden	: (solidify)
6. oblique	:linear	::luxury	: (staple)
7. apparent	:obscured	::unconcerned	: (anxious)
8. verdure	:greenery	::flawless	: (unsmirched)
9. tangible	:perceptible	::superiority	: (supremacy)
10. meek	:daring	::dishonest	: (incorruptible)

EXERCISE 5

The Master Words in this lesson are repeated below. From the Master Words, choose the appropriate word for the blank in each of the following sentences. Write the word in the numbered space provided at the right.

anxious	incorruptible	sneer	staple	unsmirched
formative	perpetuation	solidify	supremacy	vanity

1. For better or worse, during their ...?... years, children are influenced by parents. 1. (formative)
2. Rice is (a, an) ...?... in the diet of most Orientals. 2. (staple)
3. Is the ...?... of basketball as the best-attended high school sports event unchallenged? 3. (supremacy)
4. Water will ...?... as ice when the temperature drops to 32 degrees Fahrenheit. 4. (solidify)
5. The ...?... mother looked on helplessly at her son pinned under the wreckage. 5. (anxious)
6. In *All the King's Men*, Willie Stark said that no man is ...?..., that every man has his price. 6. (incorruptible)
7. Few Hollywood celebrities escape a career with their reputations ...?... . 7. (unsmirched)
8. Taking pictures and developing them immediately to the delight of the subject is sometimes called "instant ...?... ." 8. (vanity)
9. (A, An) ...?... is worthy only of mustachioed villains in old-time melodramas. 9. (sneer)
10. Of all human endeavor, the easiest is ...?... of rumor. 10. (perpetuation)

EXERCISE 6

Fill in the chart below with the Master Word that fits each set of clues. Part of speech refers to the word's usage in the lesson. Use a dictionary when necessary.

Number of Syllables	Part of Speech	Other Clues	Master Word
2	noun	bread or milk	1. (staple)
5	adjective	the way politicians should be	2. (incorruptible)
2	adjective	a perfect record is this	3. (unsmirched)
4	noun	goal of king of the mountain	4. (supremacy)
2	adjective	worrywarts are this	5. (anxious)
5	noun	vicious circle	6. (perpetuation)
4	verb	water or values might do this	7. (solidify)
3	adjective	like clay	8. (formative)
3	noun	love of self	9. (vanity)
1	verb	offer a snide remark, for example	10. (sneer)

LESSON 29

Read the following selection to get the general meaning. Read it a second time, paying special attention to the words in dark type. Notice how they are used in sentences. These are Master Words. These are the words you will be working with in this lesson.

From **The Scarlet Letter**
by Nathaniel Hawthorne

Had there been a **Papist** among the crowd of Puritans, he might have seen in this beautiful woman, so picturesque in her attire and mien, and with the infant at her bosom, an object to remind him of the image of Divine Maternity, which so many **illustrious** painters have **vied** with one another to represent; something which should remind him, indeed, but only by contrast, of that sacred image of sinless motherhood, whose infant was to **redeem** the world. Here, there was the **taint** of deepest sin in the most sacred quality of human life, working such effect, that the world was only the darker for this woman's beauty, and the more lost for the infant that she had borne.

The scene was not without a mixture of **awe**, such as must always invest the spectacle of guilt and shame in a fellow-creature, before society shall have grown **corrupt** enough to smile, instead of shuddering, at it. The witnesses of Hester Prynne's disgrace had not yet passed beyond their simplicity. They were **stern** enough to look upon her death, had that been the sentence, without a murmur at its severity, but had none of the heartlessness of another social state, which would find only a theme for jest in an exhibition like the present. Even had there been a **disposition** to turn the matter into ridicule, it must have been **repressed** and overpowered by the solemn presence of men no less dignified than the Governor, and several of his counsellors, a judge, a general and the ministers of the town. . . .

EXERCISE 1

SELF-TEST: After reading the above selection, do the following. Look at the Master Words below. Underline the words that you think you know. Circle the words that you are less sure about. Draw a square around the words you don't recognize.

MASTER WORDS

awe	**redeem**
corrupt	**repress**
disposition	**stern**
illustrious	**taint**
papist	**vie**

EXERCISE 2

Read the selection on the preceding page again, this time paying special attention to the ten Master Words. In the (a) spaces provided below, write down what you think is the meaning of the word. After you have attempted a definition for each word, look up the word in a dictionary. In the (b) spaces, copy the appropriate dictionary definition.

1. **awe** (n.)

   a. ______________________________

   b. fear; dread; amazement; wonder

2. **corrupt** (adj.)

   a. ______________________________

   b. tarnished; evil; rotten

3. **disposition** (n.)

   a. ______________________________

   b. a natural tendency or prevailing mood

4. **illustrious** (adj.)

   a. ______________________________

   b. famous, usually as a result of outstanding achievement

5. **papist** (n.)

   a. ______________________________

   b. a supporter of the pope (often a disparaging term)

6. **redeem** (v.)

   a. ______________________________

   b. to make amends or act to win forgiveness; to save from sin

7. **repress** (v.)

   a. ______________________________

   b. to quell; to restrain heavily; to keep down by force

8. **stern** (adj.)

   a. ______________________________

   b. severe or hard; unrelenting in appearance and manner; humorless

9. **taint** (n.)

   a. ______________________________

   b. stain; bare suggestion of sin and corruption; imperfection

10. **vie** (v.)

    a. ______________________________

    b. to attempt; to strive; to compete

EXERCISE 3

Use the following list of synonyms and antonyms to fill in the blanks. Some words have no antonyms. In such cases, the antonym blanks have been marked with an X.

atone	debased	profane	smiling
Catholic	disinclination	protestant	stain
compete	famous	purity	tendency
concede	liberate	restrain	unblemished
contempt	obscure	severe	wonderment

	Synonyms	Antonyms
1. **disposition**	(tendency)	(disinclination)
2. **illustrious**	(famous)	(obscure)
3. **vie**	(compete)	(concede)
4. **redeem**	(atone)	(profane)
5. **taint**	(stain)	(purity)
6. **awe**	(wonderment)	(contempt)
7. **corrupt**	(debased)	(unblemished)
8. **stern**	(severe)	(smiling)
9. **papist**	(Catholic)	(protestant)
10. **repress**	(restrain)	(liberate)

EXERCISE 4

Decide whether the first pair in the items below are synonyms or antonyms. Then choose the Master Word that shows a similar relation to the word(s) preceding the blank.

1. unsmirched	:unsoiled	::Catholic	: (papist)
2. formative	:moldable	::amazement	: (awe)
3. vanity	:humbleness	::yield	: (vie)
4. incorruptible	:unprincipled	::unknown	: (illustrious)
5. supremacy	:mastery	::save	: (redeem)
6. perpetuation	:maintenance	::strict	: (stern)
7. sneer	:compliment	::pure	: (corrupt)
8. solidify	:melt	::release	: (repress)
9. staple	:nonessential	::spotlessness	: (taint)
10. anxious	:worried	::mood	: (disposition)

EXERCISE 5

The Master Words in this lesson are repeated below. From the Master Words, choose the appropriate word for the blank in each of the following sentences. Write the word in the numbered space provided at the right.

awe	disposition	papist	repress	taint
corrupt	illustrious	redeem	stern	vie

1. Judges look ...?... to preserve the dignity of the court. — 1. (stern)
2. No ...?... of scandal had ever touched the previous city administration. — 2. (taint)
3. Leaders who ...?... the rights of others become victims of a backlash. — 3. (repress)
4. A humorous ...?... cures more problems than it causes. — 4. (disposition)
5. To most toastmasters, the guest of honor is always "...?... ." — 5. (illustrious)
6. The two candidates are expected to ...?... for the heavy Democratic vote in the third ward. — 6. (vie)
7. Hawthorne's New England background was a most likely reason for him to use the unfortunate epithet "...?..." in a religious reference. — 7. (papist)
8. The children gazed in ...?... at the Fourth of July fireworks crackling across the jet sky. — 8. (awe)
9. You can ...?... your trading stamps for valuable prizes. — 9. (redeem)
10. Polluters ...?... the environment. — 10. (corrupt)

EXERCISE 6

To complete this puzzle, fill in the Master Word associated with each phrase below. Then unscramble the circled letters to form a Master Word from Lesson 28, and define it.

1. like a hero's career — i l (l) u s t r i o u s
2. bribe taker — c o r r u (p) t
3. a cold glare — s t (e) r n
4. a sin or flaw — t (a) i n t
5. can be sunny or ugly — d i s p o (s) i t i o n
6. one who attends Mass — p a p i s (t)
7. a miracle may produce this — a w e
8. opponents do this — v i e
9. to hide your feelings — r e p r e s s
10. what some hope good deeds will do — r e d e e m

Unscrambled word: (staple)

Definition: (an essential; a necessity)

(Note: Definition may vary.)

LESSON 30

Read the following selection to get the general meaning. Read it a second time, paying special attention to the words in dark type. Notice how they are used in sentences. These are Master Words. These are the words you will be working with in this lesson.

From "**Rip Van Winkle**"
by Washington Irving

Times grew worse and worse with Rip Van Winkle as years of matrimony rolled on; a **tart** temper never **mellows** with age, and a sharp tongue is the only edged tool that grows keener with constant use. For a long while he used to **console** himself, when driven from home, by frequenting a kind of perpetual club of the sages, philosophers, and other idle **personages** of the village, which held its sessions on a bench before a small inn, designated by a **rubicund** portrait of His Majesty George the Third. Here they used to sit in the shade through a long lazy summer's day, talking **listlessly** over village gossip, or telling endless sleepy stories about nothing. But it would have been worth any statesman's money to have heard the profound discussions that sometimes took place when, by chance, an old newspaper fell into their hands from some passing traveller. How solemnly they would listen to the contents as **drawled** out by Derrick Van Bummel, the schoolmaster, a **dapper**, learned little man, who was not to be **daunted** by the most gigantic word in the dictionary; and how sagely they would **deliberate** upon public events some months after they had taken place.

EXERCISE 1

SELF-TEST: After reading the above selection, do the following. Look at the Master Words below. Underline the words that you think you know. Circle the words that you are less sure about. Draw a square around the words you don't recognize.

MASTER WORDS	
console	**listless**
dapper	**mellow**
daunt	**personage**
deliberate	**rubicund**
drawl	**tart**

EXERCISE 2

Read the selection on the preceding page again, this time paying special attention to the ten Master Words. In the (a) spaces provided below, write down what you think is the meaning of the word. After you have attempted a definition for each word, look up the word in a dictionary. In the (b) spaces, copy the appropriate dictionary definition.

1. **console** (v.)

   a. ______________________

   b. to extend comfort; to smooth over; to end distress

2. **dapper** (adj.)

   a. ______________________

   b. stylish; modern; neat; trim

3. **daunt** (v.)

   a. ______________________

   b. to frighten; to intimidate; to subdue by fear

4. **deliberate** (v.)

   a. ______________________

   b. to plan carefully and with specific intent

5. **drawl** (v.)

   a. ______________________

   b. to speak slowly in a drawn-out manner

6. **listless** (adj.)

   a. ______________________

   b. without energy; sluggish; not spirited or peppy

7. **mellow** (v.)

   a. ______________________

   b. to mature; to relax; to soften

8. **personage** (n.)

   a. ______________________

   b. a person or people in general

9. **rubicund** (adj.)

   a. ______________________

   b. red; ruddy; rosy

10. **tart** (adj.)

    a. ______________________

    b. sharp or sarcastic

EXERCISE 3

Use the following list of synonyms and antonyms to fill in the blanks. Some words have no antonyms. In such cases, the antonym blanks have been marked with an X.

brisk	embolden	neat	sharpen
chatter	improvise	pale	soften
comfort	individual	ruddy	sweet
discuss	intimidate	ruffle	unstylish
elongate	languid	sharp	

	Synonyms	Antonyms
1. **tart**	(sharp)	(sweet)
2. **mellow**	(soften)	(sharpen)
3. **console**	(comfort)	(ruffle)
4. **personage**	(individual)	X
5. **rubicund**	(ruddy)	(pale)
6. **listless**	(languid)	(brisk)
7. **drawl**	(elongate)	(chatter)
8. **dapper**	(neat)	(unstylish)
9. **daunt**	(intimidate)	(embolden)
10. **deliberate**	(discuss)	(improvise)

EXERCISE 4

Decide whether the first pair in the items below are synonyms or antonyms. Then choose the Master Word that shows a similar relation to the word(s) preceding the blank.

1. repress	:subdue	::somebody	: (personage)
2. disposition	:inclination	::frighten	: (daunt)
3. stern	:genial	::energetic	: (listless)
4. corrupt	:unsmirched	::worry	: (console)
5. papist	:Catholic	::rosy	: (rubicund)
6. redeem	:rescue	::consider	: (deliberate)
7. awe	:astonishment	::speak slowly	: (drawl)
8. vie	:surrender	::pleasant	: (tart)
9. illustrious	:insignificant	::messy	: (dapper)
10. taint	:stainlessness	::toughen	: (mellow)

EXERCISE 5

The Master Words in this lesson are repeated below. From the Master Words, choose the appropriate word for the blank in each of the following sentences. Write the word in the numbered space provided at the right.

console	daunt	drawl	mellow	rubicund
dapper	deliberate	listless	personage	tart

1. It would take more than cold to ...?... the spirits of the skiers. 1. (daunt)
2. In the first half, as we trailed 48-30, everyone agreed our team seemed ...?... . 2. (listless)
3. Roger was another victim of Mary's ...?... replies that always left deep scars. 3. (tart)
4. The superintendent of the school was now more ...?..., and the infractions that upset him years ago now seemed only boyish pranks. 4. (mellow)
5. In his knit suit and his little bow tie, affecting Hollywood shades, he looked quite ...?... as he swung along the boulevard. 5. (dapper)
6. No less a ...?... than the mayor has endorsed the bond issue. 6. (personage)
7. The jury will often ...?... for days on an important case before reaching a verdict. 7. (deliberate)
8. Mothers must ...?... children who have fallen victim to youthful tragedies—broken toys and stubbed toes. 8. (console)
9. The rim of the ...?... sun disappeared amid streaks of purple and gold. 9. (rubicund)
10. Hollywood cowboys learn to ...?... their "Howdys" and their "Good morning, ma'ams." 10. (drawl)

EXERCISE 6

To complete the word spiral, choose the Master Word associated with each phrase below. Start with 1 and fill in each answer clockwise. Be careful! Each new word may overlap the previous word by one or more letters.

1. throw a scare into
2. criticism may be this way
3. to give aid and comfort
4. people may do this with age
5. red-faced, maybe
6. some Southerners speak with this
7. lack of sleep may make you this way
8. think over carefully
9. a natty dresser, for example
10. you are one

1. D	A	U	N	2. T	A	R	T
N	6. D	R	A	W	7. L	I	3. C
U	A	T	E	9. D	A	S	O
C	R	A	G	E	P	T	N
I	E	N			10. P	L	S
B	B	O	S	R	E	E	O
U	I	L	E	8. D	S	S	L
5. R	W	O	L	L	E	4. M	E

LESSON 31

Read the following selection to get the general meaning. Read it a second time, paying special attention to the words in dark type. Notice how they are used in sentences. These are Master Words. These are the words you will be working with in this lesson.

From "**The Stout Gentleman**"
by Washington Irving

As I hate **squabbles**, particularly with women, and above all with pretty women, I **slunk** back into my room, and partly closed the door; but my curiosity was too much excited not to listen. The landlady marched intrepidly to the enemy's **citadel**, and entered it with a storm: the door closed after her. I heard her voice in a high windy **clamor** for a moment or two. Then it gradually **subsided**, like a gust of wind in a **garret**; then there was a laugh; then I heard nothing more.

After a little while my landlady came out with an odd smile on her face, **adjusting** her cap, which was a little on one side. As she went downstairs, I heard the landlord ask her what was the matter; she said, "Nothing at all, only the girl's a fool." I was more than ever **perplexed** what to make of this **unaccountable** personage, who could put a good-natured chambermaid in a passion, and send away a termagant landlady in smiles. He could not be so old, nor cross, nor ugly either.

I had to go to work at his picture again, and to paint him entirely different. I now set him down for one of those stout gentlemen that are frequently met with swaggering about the doors of country inns. Moist, merry fellows, whose bulk is a little assisted by malt-liquors. Men who have seen the world, and who are used to tavern-life. . . . Free-livers on a small scale; who are as **prodigal** as you can be with just a little money; who call all the waiters by name, tease the maids, gossip with the landlady at the bar, and philosophize over a pint of port. . . .

EXERCISE 1

SELF-TEST: After reading the above selection, do the following. Look at the Master Words below. Underline the words that you think you know. Circle the words that you are less sure about. Draw a square around the words you don't recognize.

MASTER WORDS

adjust	**prodigal**
citadel	**slink**
clamor	**squabble**
garret	**subside**
perplex	**unaccountable**

EXERCISE 2

Read the selection on the preceding page again, this time paying special attention to the ten Master Words. In the (a) spaces provided below, write down what you think is the meaning of the word. After you have attempted a definition for each word, look up the word in a dictionary. In the (b) spaces, copy the appropriate dictionary definition.

1. **adjust** (v.)

   a. __________

   b. to set right; to fit; to regulate

2. **citadel** (n.)

   a. __________

   b. fortress; stronghold

3. **clamor** (n.)

   a. __________

   b. outburst of sound; loud cry; noise of discontent

4. **garret** (n.)

   a. __________

   b. attic; part of house immediately under roof

5. **perplex** (v.)

   a. __________

   b. to puzzle; to confuse; to complicate

6. **prodigal** (adj.)

   a. __________

   b. wasteful; thriftless

7. **slink** (v.)

   a. __________

   b. to move in stealth and silence; to lurk

8. **squabble** (n.)

   a. __________

   b. a quarrel, sometimes short-lived and of little importance

9. **subside** (v.)

   a. __________

   b. to abate; to lessen in intensity; to ebb

10. **unaccountable** (adj.)

    a. __________

    b. not capable of explanation; mysterious

EXERCISE 3

Use the following list of synonyms and antonyms to fill in the blanks. Some words have no antonyms. In such cases, the antonym blanks have been marked with an X.

argument	edify	harmony	sneak
attic	explainable	increase	strut
cellar	fix	mysterious	uproar
disarrange	fortress	puzzle	wasteful
ebb	frugal	silence	

	Synonyms	Antonyms
1. **squabble**	(argument)	(harmony)
2. **slink**	(sneak)	(strut)
3. **citadel**	(fortress)	X
4. **clamor**	(uproar)	(silence)
5. **subside**	(ebb)	(increase)
6. **garret**	(attic)	(cellar)
7. **adjust**	(fix)	(disarrange)
8. **perplex**	(puzzle)	(edify)
9. **unaccountable**	(mysterious)	(explainable)
10. **prodigal**	(wasteful)	(frugal)

EXERCISE 4

Decide whether the first pair in the items below are synonyms or antonyms. Then choose the Master Word that shows a similar relation to the word(s) preceding the blank.

1. personage	:being	::creep	: (slink)
2. daunt	:unnerve	::stronghold	: (citadel)
3. tart	:gracious	::definable	: (unaccountable)
4. deliberate	:plan	::loft	: (garret)
5. listless	:lively	::agreement	: (squabble)
6. drawl	:lengthen	::regulate	: (adjust)
7. mellow	:harden	::rise	: (subside)
8. dapper	:tacky	::clarify	: (perplex)
9. rubicund	:florid	::extravagant	: (prodigal)
10. console	:upset	::quiet	: (clamor)

EXERCISE 5

The Master Words in this lesson are repeated below. From the Master Words, choose the appropriate word for the blank in each of the following sentences. Write the word in the numbered space provided at the right.

adjust	clamor	perplex	slink	subside
citadel	garret	prodigal	squabble	unaccountable

1. For maximum gas mileage, ...?... the carburetor frequently. — 1. (adjust)
2. The ...?... disappearance of the diplomat caused great alarm. — 2. (unaccountable)
3. The early artist was frequently portrayed starving in (a, an) ...?... . — 3. (garret)
4. After winds of 100 miles per hour, the hurricane began to ...?... . — 4. (subside)
5. The thrifty ant is more likely to survive the tough winters than the more ...?... grasshopper. — 5. (prodigal)
6. After the fourth straight loss of the season, there was (a, an) ...?... for the coach's resignation. — 6. (clamor)
7. The ...?... is near the Plains of Abraham, looking out over Quebec Harbor in a position for strategic defense. — 7. (citadel)
8. Cowardly coyotes ...?... low over the sage in search of their prey. — 8. (slink)
9. Computer logic is certain to ...?... those uninitiated to order and routine. — 9. (perplex)
10. The predictable ...?... over toys broke out when the children began to play. — 10. (squabble)

EXERCISE 6

The invented words below are formed from parts of different Master Words from this lesson. Create a definition and indicate the part of speech for each word. The first one is done for you.

squabbleplex *(v.) to confuse by arguing over something trivial*

citaslink ([v.] to sneak into an enemy fortress)

unaccountaplex ([n.] a feeling of unusual and unexplainable confusion)

prodisquabble ([n.] a quarrel over spending money wastefully)

Now invent your own words by combining parts of the Master Words. Create a definition for each, and indicate the word's part of speech. (You may reuse any of the word parts above in new combinations.)

1. ____________ ____________________________

2. ____________ ____________________________

(Note: Answers will vary.)

Other possibilities:
citaclamor (n.) the noise that accompanies an attack on a fortress
prodislink (v.) to return in shame after squandering one's money
squabadjust (v.) to become accustomed to petty quarrels

LESSON 32

Read the following selection to get the general meaning. Read it a second time, paying special attention to the words in dark type. Notice how they are used in sentences. These are Master Words. These are the words you will be working with in this lesson.

From "**Rip Van Winkle**"
by Washington Irving

It is a little village of great **antiquity**, having been founded by some of the Dutch colonists in the early times of the province. . . .

He [Rip Van Winkle] was a descendant of the Van Winkles who figured so **gallantly** in the **chivalrous** days of Peter Stuyvesant, and accompanied him to the **siege** of Fort Christina. He inherited, however, but little of the martial character of his ancestors. I have observed that he was a simple good-natured man; he was, moreover, a kind neighbor, and an obedient, hen-pecked husband. Indeed, to the latter circumstance might be owing that meekness of spirit which gained him such universal popularity; for those men are most apt to be **obsequious** and **conciliating** abroad who are under the discipline of **shrews** at home. Their tempers, doubtless, are rendered pliant and **malleable** in the fiery furnace of domestic **tribulation**; and a curtain lecture is worth all the sermons in the world for teaching the virtues of patience and long-suffering. A termagant wife may, therefore, in some respects be considered a **tolerable** blessing; and if so, Rip Van Winkle was thrice blessed.

EXERCISE 1

SELF-TEST: After reading the above selection, do the following. Look at the Master Words below. Underline the words that you think you know. Circle the words that you are less sure about. Draw a square around the words you don't recognize.

MASTER WORDS	
antiquity	**obsequious**
chivalrous	**shrew**
conciliate	**siege**
gallant	**tolerable**
malleable	**tribulation**

EXERCISE 2

Read the selection on the preceding page again, this time paying special attention to the ten Master Words. In the (a) spaces provided below, write down what you think is the meaning of the word. After you have attempted a definition for each word, look up the word in a dictionary. In the (b) spaces, copy the appropriate dictionary definition.

1. **antiquity** (n.)
   a. __________
   b. ancientness; age; something related to time long past

2. **chivalrous** (adj.)
   a. __________
   b. civil; well-bred; courteous

3. **conciliate** (v.)
   a. __________
   b. to bring together in goodwill; to negotiate; to restore peace

4. **gallant** (adj.)
   a. __________
   b. noble; brave; heroic and spirited

5. **malleable** (adj.)
   a. __________
   b. capable of being bent or shaped; manageable

6. **obsequious** (adj.)
   a. __________
   b. fawning; subservient; overly patronizing

7. **shrew** (n.)
   a. __________
   b. a scolding, nagging woman

8. **siege** (n.)
   a. __________
   b. an attack; an extended assault

9. **tolerable** (adj.)
   a. __________
   b. can be put up with; bearable

10. **tribulation** (n.)
    a. __________
    b. struggle; distress; suffering, frequently from oppression

EXERCISE 3

Use the following list of synonyms and antonyms to fill in the blanks. Some words have no antonyms. In such cases, the antonym blanks have been marked with an X.

age	brash	noble	servile
agitate	courteous	ordeal	termagant
attack	insufferable	pacify	villainous
bearable	lady	plastic	vulgar
blessing	newness	rigid	withdrawal

	Synonyms	Antonyms
1. **antiquity**	(age)	(newness)
2. **gallant**	(noble)	(villainous)
3. **chivalrous**	(courteous)	(vulgar)
4. **siege**	(attack)	(withdrawal)
5. **obsequious**	(servile)	(brash)
6. **conciliate**	(pacify)	(agitate)
7. **shrew**	(termagant)	(lady)
8. **malleable**	(plastic)	(rigid)
9. **tribulation**	(ordeal)	(blessing)
10. **tolerable**	(bearable)	(insufferable)

EXERCISE 4

Decide whether the first pair in the items below are synonyms or antonyms. Then choose the Master Word that shows a similar relation to the word(s) preceding the blank.

1. clamor	:noise	::oldness	: (antiquity)
2. prodigal	:thrifty	::good fortune	: (tribulation)
3. adjust	:reset	::gracious	: (chivalrous)(gallant)
4. perplex	:enlighten	::provoke	: (conciliate)
5. subside	:strengthen	::disrespectful	: (obsequious)
6. garret	:attic	::nagger	: (shrew)
7. unaccountable	:understandable	::unbearable	: (tolerable)
8. citadel	:tower	::flexible	: (malleable)
9. slink	:prowl	::assault	: (siege)
10. squabble	:peace	::dishonorable	: (gallant)(chivalrous)

EXERCISE 5

The Master Words in this lesson are repeated below. From the Master Words, choose the appropriate word for the blank in each of the following sentences. Write the word in the numbered space provided at the right.

antiquity	conciliate	malleable	shrew	tolerable
chivalrous	gallant	obsequious	siege	tribulation

1. Sharp-tongued Kate is (a, an) ...?... in a well-known play by Shakespeare. 1. (shrew)
2. Odysseus was among those present at the ...?... of Troy. 2. (siege)
3. Children learn quickly because they are more ...?... than adults and less set in their ways. 3. (malleable)
4. The world will never know the ...?...(s) of the six million Jews killed by the Nazis. 4. (tribulation)
5. While the new medicine did not cure the disease, it at least made life ...?..., if not enjoyable. 5. (tolerable)
6. The ...?... little three-year-old had again demonstrated her fine blood lines when she won both major derbies. 6. (gallant)
7. Did women's lib bring to an end the ...?... acts of courtesy offered by gentlemen? 7. (chivalrous)
8. Sanskrit, the parent language of English, is a language of ...?... . 8. (antiquity)
9. ...?... persons demonstrate a lack of courage rather than an abundance of courtesy. 9. (Obsequious)
10. Big loans to foreign countries do not always ...?... those countries or change hostile attitudes. 10. (conciliate)

EXERCISE 6

To complete the crossword, choose the Master Word associated with each word or phrase below. Begin each answer in the square having the same number as the clue.

1. what Job or Uncle Tom suffered
2. bootlickers are this
3. Sir Lancelot
4. Egyptian pyramids or Dead Sea Scrolls, for example
5. bends but doesn't break
6. some situations are barely this way
7. King Arthur's men
8. storming a castle
9. what a peace summit should do
10. fault-finder

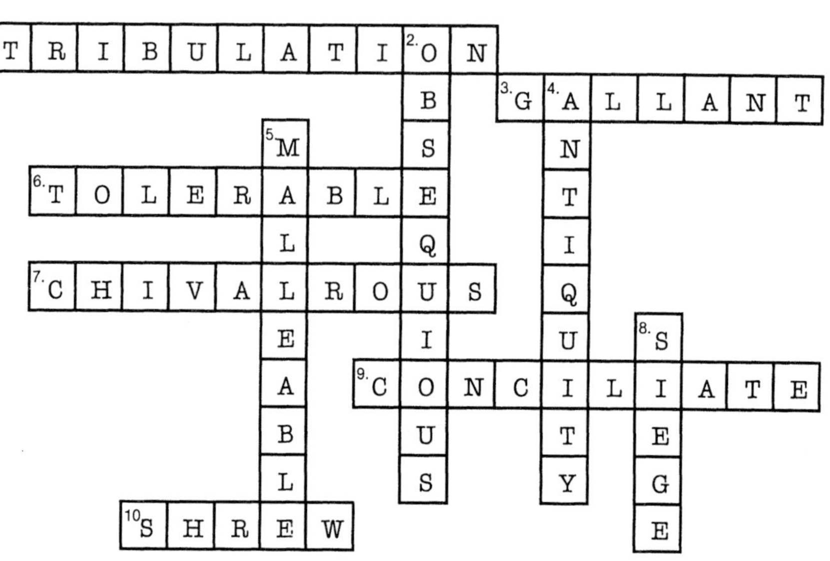

LESSON 33

Read the following selection to get the general meaning. Read it a second time, paying special attention to the words in dark type. Notice how they are used in sentences. These are Master Words. These are the words you will be working with in this lesson.

From **Wuthering Heights**
by Emily Bronte

He [Heathcliff] had reached the age of sixteen then, I think, and without having bad features or being **deficient** in intellect, he contrived to convey an impression of inward and outward repulsiveness that his present aspect retains no traces of.

In the first place, he had, by that time, lost the benefit of his early education: continual hard work, begun soon and concluded late, had **extinguished** any curiosity he once possessed in pursuit of knowledge, and any love for books, or learning. His childhood's sense of superiority, **instilled** into him by the favors of old Mr. Earnshaw, was faded away. He struggled long to keep up an equality with Catherine in her studies and yielded with **poignant** though silent regret: but, he yielded completely; and there was no prevailing on him to take a step in the way of moving upward, when he found he must, necessarily, sink beneath his former level. Then personal appearance sympathised with mental **deterioration**; he acquired a **slouching** gait, and **ignoble** look; his naturally reserved disposition was **exaggerated** into an almost idiotic excess of unsociable **moroseness**; and he took a grim pleasure, apparently, in exciting the **aversion** rather than the esteem of his few acquaintances.

EXERCISE 1

SELF-TEST: After reading the above selection, do the following. Look at the Master Words below. Underline the words that you think you know. Circle the words that you are less sure about. Draw a square around the words you don't recognize.

MASTER WORDS

aversion	**ignoble**
deficient	**instill**
deterioration	**morose**
exaggerate	**poignant**
extinguish	**slouch**

EXERCISE 2

Read the selection on the preceding page again, this time paying special attention to the ten Master Words. In the (a) spaces provided below, write down what you think is the meaning of the word. After you have attempted a definition for each word, look up the word in a dictionary. In the (b) spaces, copy the appropriate dictionary definition.

1. **aversion** (n.)
   a. ______
   b. turning away; repugnance; antipathy
2. **deficient** (adj.)
   a. ______
   b. not adequate; lacking in a quality; falling short
3. **deterioration** (n.)
   a. ______
   b. worsening of a condition
4. **exaggerate** (v.)
   a. ______
   b. to distort the truth; to increase or exceed normal; to tell "tall tales"
5. **extinguish** (v.)
   a. ______
   b. to put out, as a flame; to abolish; to do away with
6. **ignoble** (adj.)
   a. ______
   b. base; lacking honor; of low birth
7. **instill** (v.)
   a. ______
   b. to impart or indoctrinate; to add gradually
8. **morose** (adj.)
   a. ______
   b. sullen; brooding; disagreeably sorrowful
9. **poignant** (adj.)
   a. ______
   b. sharp; painful emotionally; piercing; causing deep feeling
10. **slouch** (v.)
    a. ______
    b. to slope; to walk lazily with head and shoulders stooped

EXERCISE 3

Use the following list of synonyms and antonyms to fill in the blanks. Some words have no antonyms. In such cases, the antonym blanks have been marked with an X.

abundant	cheerful	imbue	purge
attraction	decay	lacking	recovery
avoidance	gloomy	minimize	smother
base	honorable	overstate	stoop
bland	ignite	piteous	strut

	Synonyms	Antonyms
1. **deficient**	(lacking)	(abundant)
2. **extinguish**	(smother)	(ignite)
3. **instill**	(imbue)	(purge)
4. **poignant**	(piteous)	(bland)
5. **deterioration**	(decay)	(recovery)
6. **slouch**	(stoop)	(strut)
7. **ignoble**	(base)	(honorable)
8. **exaggerate**	(overstate)	(minimize)
9. **morose**	(gloomy)	(cheerful)
10. **aversion**	(avoidance)	(attraction)

EXERCISE 4

Decide whether the first pair in the items below are synonyms or antonyms. Then choose the Master Word that shows a similar relation to the word(s) preceding the blank.

1. tolerable	:impossible	::dull	: (poignant)
2. antiquity	:modernism	::lessen	: (exaggerate)
3. siege	:storm	::impart	: (instill)
4. gallant	:villainous	::respectable	: (ignoble)
5. chivalrous	:noble	::opposition	: (aversion)
6. shrew	:lady	::upbeat	: (morose)
7. tribulation	:suffering	::slump	: (slouch)
8. malleable	:formative	::incomplete	: (deficient)
9. conciliate	:upset	::light	: (extinguish)
10. obsequious	:groveling	::decline	: (deterioration)

EXERCISE 5

The Master Words in this lesson are repeated below. From the Master Words, choose the appropriate word for the blank in each of the following sentences. Write the word in the numbered space provided at the right.

aversion	deterioration	extinguish	instill	poignant
deficient	exaggerate	ignoble	morose	slouch

1. Parents tend to ...?... in their children respect for others. 1. (instill)
2. Firefighters were able to ...?... the blaze in only minutes. 2. (extinguish)
3. Unfortunately, psychologists seldom see patients until ...?... of personality has already begun. 3. (deterioration)
4. Hyperbole is a kind of literary humor created when the author ...?...(s) a situation, event, or person. 4. (exaggerate)
5. Colds are more likely to happen when you are ...?... in vitamin C. 5. (deficient)
6. When you get older, it is said that the most ...?... memories are of childhood Christmases. 6. (poignant)
7. Some teachers encourage students who ...?... to sit up straight in their seats. 7. (slouch)
8. Like most teen-agers, he had (a, an) ...?... to study most evident when a good movie was in town. 8. (aversion)
9. Such ...?... behavior is expected from a rascal like you! 9. (ignoble)
10. During his illness, he became ...?..., rarely speaking to anyone. 10. (morose)

EXERCISE 6

Order the words in each item from *least* to *most.* Use the abbreviations *L* for "least" and *M* for "most." Leave the line before the word of the middle degree blank. The first word provides a clue about how to arrange the words. See the example.

forbidden: M outlawed L legal ___discouraged
(*Legal* indicates the least forbidden; *outlawed* indicates the most forbidden.)

1. value:	___deficient	(L) worthless	(M) satisfactory
2. interference:	___prevent	(M) extinguish	(L) discourage
3. ruin:	(L) neglect	(M) collapse	___deterioration
4. dislike:	(M) hatred	___aversion	(L) indifference
5. dishonest:	(M) lie	(L) confess	___exaggerate
6. sullen:	(L) withdrawn	(M) morose	___cranky
7. stimulating:	(M) poignant	___touching	(L) dull
8. forceful:	___instill	(L) offer	(M) brainwash
9. refined:	(L) ignoble	___mannerly	(M) cultured
10. disciplined:	(L) slouch	___exercise	(M) drill

(Note: In some cases, answers may vary.)

LESSON 34

Read the following selection to get the general meaning. Read it a second time, paying special attention to the words in dark type. Notice how they are used in sentences. These are Master Words. These are the words you will be working with in this lesson.

From **Jane Eyre**
by Charlotte Bronte

John Reed was a schoolboy of fourteen years old; four years older than I, for I was but ten; large and **stout** for his age, with a dingy and **unwholesome** skin; thick **lineaments** in a **spacious** visage, heavy limbs and large **extremities**. He **gorged** himself **habitually** at table, which made him **bilious**, and gave him a dim and bleared eye and flabby cheeks. He ought now to have been at school; but his mama had taken him home for a month or two, "on account of his **delicate** health." Mr. Miles, the master, **affirmed** that he would do very well if he had fewer cakes and sweetmeats sent him from home, but the mother's heart turned from an opinion so harsh, and inclined rather to the more refined idea that John's sallowness was owing to over-application and, perhaps, to pining after home.

EXERCISE 1

SELF-TEST: After reading the above selection, do the following. Look at the Master Words below. Underline the words that you think you know. Circle the words that you are less sure about. Draw a square around the words you don't recognize.

MASTER WORDS	
affirm	**habitual**
bilious	**lineaments**
delicate	**spacious**
extremity	**stout**
gorge	**unwholesome**

EXERCISE 2

Read the selection on the preceding page again, this time paying special attention to the ten Master Words. In the (a) spaces provided below, write down what you think is the meaning of the word. After you have attempted a definition for each word, look up the word in a dictionary. In the (b) spaces, copy the appropriate dictionary definition.

1. **affirm** (v.)

   a. ______________________

   b. to assert; to give testimony; to support by statement

2. **bilious** (adj.)

   a. ______________________

   b. ill-tempered or out of sorts

3. **delicate** (adj.)

   a. ______________________

   b. fragile; frail

4. **extremity** (n.)

   a. ______________________

   b. the end of a limb, generally meaning hands and feet

5. **gorge** (v.)

   a. ______________________

   b. to stuff; to fill; to eat with considerable greed

6. **habitual** (adj.)

   a. ______________________

   b. automatic; learned through repetition

7. **lineaments** (n.)

   a. ______________________

   b. features, especially on the face

8. **spacious** (adj.)

   a. ______________________

   b. large; roomy

9. **stout** (adj.)

   a. ______________________

   b. sturdy; solid; substantial

10. **unwholesome** (adj.)

    a. ______________________

    b. not healthful physically, spiritually, or morally

EXERCISE 3

Use the following list of synonyms and antonyms to fill in the blanks. Some words have no antonyms. In such cases, the antonym blanks have been marked with an X.

affable	famish	profile	salubrious
assert	featurelessness	puny	stuff
cramped	foot	regular	sturdy
deny	fragile	roomy	torso
erratic	irritable	rugged	toxic

	Synonyms	Antonyms
1. **stout**	(rugged) (sturdy)	(puny)
2. **unwholesome**	(toxic)	(salubrious)
3. **lineaments**	(profile)	(featurelessness)
4. **spacious**	(roomy)	(cramped)
5. **extremity**	(foot)	(torso)
6. **gorge**	(stuff)	(famish)
7. **habitual**	(regular)	(erratic)
8. **bilious**	(irritable)	(affable)
9. **delicate**	(fragile)	(sturdy) (rugged)
10. **affirm**	(assert)	(deny)

EXERCISE 4

Decide whether the first pair in the items below are synonyms or antonyms. Then choose the Master Word that shows a similar relation to the word(s) preceding the blank.

1. morose	:sunny	::small	: (spacious)
2. instill	:indoctrinate	::features	: (lineaments)
3. exaggerate	:diminish	::cheerful	: (bilious)
4. deterioration	:worsening	::cram	: (gorge)
5. slouch	:droop	::solid	: (stout)
6. extinguish	:burn	::strong	: (delicate)
7. poignant	:unmoving	::healthful	: (unwholesome)
8. ignoble	:distinguished	::irregular	: (habitual)
9. aversion	:repulsion	::declare	: (affirm)
10. deficient	:inadequate	::finger	: (extremity)

EXERCISE 5

The Master Words in this lesson are repeated below. From the Master Words, choose the appropriate word for the blank in each of the following sentences. Write the word in the numbered space provided at the right.

affirm	delicate	gorge	lineaments	stout
bilious	extremity	habitual	spacious	unwholesome

1. ...?... traffic violators may lose their licenses. 1. (Habitual)
2. On the first day of work at the candy counter, you are likely to ...?... yourself. 2. (gorge)
3. Indigestion may make a person ...?... . 3. (bilious)
4. Reciting the oath allows club members to ...?... their purpose. 4. (affirm)
5. Even though our textile art is superior, we cannot seem to weave fabric as ...?... as a spider web. 5. (delicate)
6. Exposure to bitter cold may cause (a, an) ...?... to become frostbitten. 6. (extremity)
7. The ...?... Forum is an ideal place to play a basketball game where a crowd of 15,000 is expected. 7. (spacious)
8. I tried to study the ...?... of Ethan's face, but he turned his head away. 8. (lineaments)
9. Diets which do not have a proper balance of fats, proteins, and carbohydrates are ...?... . 9. (unwholesome)
10. The heavy computer required (a, an) ...?... table to bear its weight. 10. (stout)

EXERCISE 6

Fill in the chart below with the Master Word that fits each set of clues. Part of speech refers to the word's usage in the lesson. Use a dictionary when necessary.

Number of Syllables	Part of Speech	Other Clues	Master Word
2	adjective	with room to breathe	1. (spacious)
2	verb	to declare solemnly	2. (affirm)
4	noun	your hand, for example	3. (extremity)
1	verb	what a dieter can't do	4. (gorge)
4	noun	what a portrait captures	5. (lineaments)
3	adjective	like a newborn baby	6. (delicate)
4	adjective	what brushing your teeth should be	7. (habitual)
2	adjective	out of sorts	8. (bilious)
3	adjective	not good for you	9. (unwholesome)
1	adjective	not a 90-pound weakling	10. (stout)

LESSON 35

Read the following selection to get the general meaning. Read it a second time, paying special attention to the words in dark type. Notice how they are used in sentences. These are Master Words. These are the words you will be working with in this lesson.

From a speech by John N. Mitchell (1970)

But Constitutional rights in themselves are meaningless without legislation to **implement** them, an Executive to carry them out and courts to interpret them. . . .

We can afford some popular cynicism about the Legislature and the Executive. They are subject to the **mandate** of the **electorate**. They are frequently involved in **partisan** politics and our citizens often have a healthy **skepticism** for the pronouncements and motivations of politicians. . . .

It may be suggested by some that an official of the Executive Branch is perhaps overstepping the bounds of **propriety** by commenting so directly on the activities of the Judiciary.

But I believe that recent events have **imposed** upon me the obligation as Attorney General to give my own defense of the Supreme Court and to call for an end to irresponsible and **malicious** criticism which will not only damage the Supreme Court but will **undermine** all of our courts and our respect for our system of laws.

In so doing, I beg the forgiveness of the Judiciary if my comments are interpreted in any **adverse** manner.

EXERCISE 1

SELF-TEST: After reading the above selection, do the following. Look at the Master Words below. Underline the words that you think you know. Circle the words that you are less sure about. Draw a square around the words you don't recognize.

MASTER WORDS	
adverse	**mandate**
electorate	**partisan**
implement	**propriety**
impose	**skepticism**
malicious	**undermine**

EXERCISE 2

Read the selection on the preceding page again, this time paying special attention to the ten Master Words. In the (a) spaces provided below, write down what you think is the meaning of the word. After you have attempted a definition for each word, look up the word in a dictionary. In the (b) spaces, copy the appropriate dictionary definition.

1. **adverse** (adj.)

   a. ______________________________

   b. against; not favorable; antagonistic

2. **electorate** (n.)

   a. ______________________________

   b. voters; constituents

3. **implement** (v.)

   a. ______________________________

   b. to bring about; to fulfill an action; to activate what was an idea

4. **impose** (v.)

   a. ______________________________

   b. to press or force upon; to charge or place upon

5. **malicious** (adj.)

   a. ______________________________

   b. wicked; evil; intending to do wrong

6. **mandate** (n.)

   a. ______________________________

   b. an order, instruction, or authority given by constituents

7. **partisan** (adj.)

   a. ______________________________

   b. exhibiting partiality or loyalty to one cause

8. **propriety** (n.)

   a. ______________________________

   b. sense of what is appropriate or proper

9. **skepticism** (n.)

   a. ______________________________

   b. state of doubt; disbelief; questioning attitude

10. **undermine** (v.)

    a. ______________________________

    b. to weaken or ruin gradually another's health or reputation

EXERCISE 3

Use the following list of synonyms and antonyms to fill in the blanks. Some words have no antonyms. In such cases, the antonym blanks have been marked with an X.

activate	faith	order	spiteful
benign	inappropriateness	partial	support
constituents	intrude	propitious	unfavorable
decorum	neutral	renunciation	vegetate
doubt	nonvoters	sabotage	withhold

	Synonyms	Antonyms
1. **implement**	(activate)	(vegetate)
2. **mandate**	(order)	(renunciation)
3. **electorate**	(constituents)	(nonvoters)
4. **partisan**	(partial)	(neutral)
5. **skepticism**	(doubt)	(faith)
6. **propriety**	(decorum)	(inappropriateness)
7. **impose**	(intrude)	(withhold)
8. **malicious**	(spiteful)	(benign)
9. **undermine**	(sabotage)	(support)
10. **adverse**	(unfavorable)	(propitious)

EXERCISE 4

Decide whether the first pair in the items below are synonyms or antonyms. Then choose the Master Word that shows a similar relation to the word(s) preceding the blank.

1. unwholesome	:nourishing	::trust	: (skepticism)
2. bilious	:good-natured	::refrain	: (impose)
3. delicate	:tough	::kind	: (malicious)
4. extremity	:hand	::voters	: (electorate)
5. lineaments	:looks	::command	: (mandate)
6. affirm	:testify	::harmful	: (adverse)
7. habitual	:uncustomary	::unbiased	: (partisan)
8. gorge	:overeat	::execute	: (implement)
9. stout	:husky	::damage	: (undermine)
10. spacious	:packed	::unsuitability	: (propriety)

EXERCISE 5

The Master Words in this lesson are repeated below. From the Master Words, choose the appropriate word for the blank in each of the following sentences. Write the word in the numbered space provided at the right.

adverse	implement	malicious	partisan	skepticism
electorate	impose	mandate	propriety	undermine

1. Moral conscience should tell us not to ...?... our way of life on other countries. 1. (impose)
2. Breaking the window led to a charge of ...?... mischief filed by police. 2. (malicious)
3. Every President has a standing ...?... to increase government benefits and lower taxes, but no one believes it will happen. 3. (mandate)
4. ...?... fans poured out on the floor when the official called a jump ball instead of a foul. 4. (Partisan)
5. Has television had the ...?... effect on reading habits that was predicted? 5. (adverse)
6. Some members of Congress believe that they are more responsible to the ...?... than to their own consciences. 6. (electorate)
7. Glowing claims of some advertisers create more ...?... than sales. 7. (skepticism)
8. The President asked for legislation to ...?... his new program. 8. (implement)
9. Good manners come from experience in an environment where ...?... has a high priority. 9. (propriety)
10. Inattention to diet can ...?... the health of both old and young. 10. (undermine)

EXERCISE 6

To complete this puzzle, fill in the Master Word associated with each phrase below. Then unscramble the circled letters to form a Master Word from Lesson 34, and define it.

1. describes unpleasant weather — (a) d v e r s e
2. to weaken slowly — u n d (e) r m i n e
3. Doubting Thomas was filled with this — s k e p t i c (i) s m
4. "the people have spoken" — m a n (d) a t e
5. like one who votes a straight-party ticket — p a r t i s a n
6. an etiquette book defines this — p r o p r i (e) t y
7. to put in action — i m p (l) e m e n t
8. a spiteful person is this way — m a l i (c) i o u s
9. to force your wishes on another — i m p o s e
10. the grass roots of politics — e l e c t o r a (t) e

Unscrambled word: (delicate)

Definition: (fragile, not strong)

(Note: Definition may vary.)

LESSON 36

Part I: From the list below, choose the correct word for each sentence that follows. Use each word only once.

affirm	flagrant	gorge	repress
chivalrous	forlorn	malicious	staple
extinguish	garret	prototype	tangible

1. Bread is (a, an) ___(staple)___ in most people's diet.
2. SUNCO believes its new $100 million plant will ___(affirm)___ public faith in free enterprise.
3. I failed to see any ___(tangible)___ benefits among all the hypothetical arguments advanced by the idealists.
4. They presented (a, an) ___(prototype)___ of the new mall to be built next year.
5. The girls tried to ___(repress)___ their laughter, but their muffled gasps and snorts soon caught the minister's attention.
6. Be sure to ___(extinguish)___ your campfire before breaking camp or going to sleep.
7. Starving and freezing in (a, an) ___(garret)___ may sound like a romantic way to become a poet, but it isn't much fun.
8. Can anything look more ___(forlorn)___ that a wet cat shivering in the snow?
9. With (a, an) ___(chivalrous)___ smile, the diplomat backed from the room, bowing and scraping as he went.
10. The ravenous survivors ___(gorge)___ (d, ed) themselves on the bananas and coconuts they found on the island.
11. I had never before seen so ___(flagrant)___ a violation of the rules of good sportsmanship.
12. ___(Malicious)___ little boys used to dip girls' pigtails into inkwells.

Part II: From the list below, choose the correct word for each sentence that follows. Use each word only once.

aversion	deliberate	laterally	slink
beamed	hypothesis	lopsided	tolerable
clamor	illustrious	mellow	unsmirched

1. You can move playing pieces ___(laterally)___ on the game board.
2. Senator Kaufmann's reputation remained ___(unsmirched)___ even though he was connected with the bribery scandal.
3. The ___(clamor)___ in the classroom quickly subsided when the bell rang, and the students silently began the exam.
4. The 48–0 victory was one of the most ___(lopsided)___ victories in school history.
5. The faculty met behind closed doors to ___(deliberate)___ at length on the question.

6. Lazy, easygoing Martin seemed to have (a, an) ____(aversion)____ to any hard work.

7. We weren't enthusiastic over the results, but we thought he had done (a, an) ____(tolerable)____ job, considering his inexperience and the circumstances.

8. The principal seems to have ____(mellow)____ (d, ed) since the old days when she threatened to expel any tardy students.

9. After such (a, an) ____(illustrious)____ career as a concert pianist, I don't see how he can bear to walk the streets unrecognized.

10. As their children received their medals for academic excellence, their parents ____(beamed)____.

11. Cranston felt as if he wanted to ____(slink)____ out the back door after he received a tongue-lashing from the president.

12. The scientist came up with a brilliant ____(hypothesis)____, but unfortunately his later experiments proved to be unworkable.

Part III: Decide whether the first pair in the items below are synonyms or antonyms. Then choose a Master Word from Lessons 25–35 that shows a similar relation to the word(s) preceding the blank. Do not repeat a Master Word that appears in the first column.

1. imposing	:unimpressive	::corrupt	: (redeem)
2. stocky	:husky	::confuse	: (perplex)
3. anxious	:troubled	::dishonorable	: (ignoble)
4. deficient	:plentiful	::improvement	: (deterioration)
5. intimacy	:closeness	::reassure	: (console)
6. interlaced	:woven	::excessive	: (prodigal)
7. preoccupation	:distraction	::trim	: (dapper)
8. apparent	:noticeable	::patch up	: (conciliate)
9. subside	:diminish	::formative	: (malleable)
10. sneer	:scoff	::moving	: (poignant)
11. oblique	:slanting	::assorted	: (sundry)
12. forlorn	:joyous	::remove	: (instill)
13. squabble	:fight	::frail	: (delicate)
14. daunt	:encourage	::straight	: (tilted)
15. relate	:describe	::singing	: (lilting)
16. staple	:essential	::hardship	: (tribulation)
17. vanity	:egotism	::quiet	: (muffle)
18. adverse	:favorable	::immaterial	: (tangible)
19. endeavor	:strive	::conquer	: (subdue)
20. stern	:easygoing	::pallid	: (rubicund)

(Note: Other answers may be possible.)

INDEX—Word and Lesson Number

WORD LISTS—Lessons 1–11

Lesson 1

alleviate
altruism
bestow
humanity
mendicant
perturbation
polychromatic
solace
subjugation
succor

Lesson 2

concepts
diversity
dubbed
enclaves
endearment
honorary
indelible
motto
multiculturalism
patent

Lesson 3

accessible
ascend
chafe
impetuous
impinge
pulverize
reverberate
saunter
staid
tranquil

Lesson 4

allusion
compel
concur
dispel
impute
initiative
insinuate
recollect
restraint
retort

Lesson 5

consisted
futility
haphazardly
juxtaposing
knitted
proffered
recount
sarcastic
stirring
unification

Lesson 6

ambitious
compounds
cope
knobbed
legalized
migrated
pensions
sanitary facilities
sprawling
surge

Lesson 7

curious
grim
grimy
imprecation
intervene
massacre
obliterate
onslaught
tousled
utterly

Lesson 8

eclipse
expedient
ferocity
infernal
ingenuity
persecution
reproach
revile
taunt
termination

Lesson 9

allocated
behalf
campaigns
deposit
erected
expectancy
procure
savagery
site
tolerable

Lesson 10

alter
course
derive
dissolve
endow
entitle
impel
inalienable
institute
secure

Lesson 11

firmament
generate
heath
opacity
pallid
precise
retard
tract
transitional
vast

WORD LISTS—Lessons 13–23

Lesson 13
composed
express
fragile
frantically
missionary
numbness
practical
refugee
unspeakable
version

Lesson 14
anecdote
dearth
economical
grave
infinite
mode
precarious
relieve
steer
unconscious

Lesson 15
crevice
defiance
despairingly
dismal
flawed
lament
shrill
stealthily
strive
vault

Lesson 16
achievement
cocked
dais
green
harmonic
headlong
podium
risers
trustee
whoop

Lesson 17
blight
dilapidation
immolate
indifferent
participation
picturesque
pique
temperament
venerable
verge

Lesson 18
belie
florid
fringe
glisten
intensify
jovial
limpid
perpetual
ruddy
sly

Lesson 19
arbitrate
capable
contradictory
discernment
fatigue
impulse
instinct
mute
resolve
straits

Lesson 20
anatomical
apparatus
celebrated
cupola
dingy
dissect
heir
laden
litter
strewn

Lesson 21
abstinence
alight
copious
demeanor
dispensable
inhibition
relegated
sparse
stringent
sustained

Lesson 22
aspire
exult
gaunt
impending
infirmity
kindling
precipice
recompense
susceptible
vagary

Lesson 23
audible
bewilderment
define
detach
intrepid
pulsation
stupefaction
undulate
vibration
wan

WORD LISTS—Lessons 25–35

Lesson 25

beguile
endeavor
flagrant
hypothesis
intimacy
preoccupation
prototype
relate
reminiscence
subdue

Lesson 26

beamed
flanked
forlorn
interlaced
lilting
lopsided
posture
stocky
terminal
tilted

Lesson 27

apparent
imposing
laterally
meek
muffle
oblique
sundry
tangible
treacherous
verdure

Lesson 28

anxious
formative
incorruptible
perpetuation
sneer
solidify
staple
supremacy
unsmirched
vanity

Lesson 29

awe
corrupt
disposition
illustrious
papist
redeem
repress
stern
taint
vie

Lesson 30

console
dapper
daunt
deliberate
drawl
listless
mellow
personage
rubicund
tart

Lesson 31

adjust
citadel
clamor
garret
perplex
prodigal
slink
squabble
subside
unaccountable

Lesson 32

antiquity
chivalrous
conciliate
gallant
malleable
obsequious
shrew
siege
tolerable
tribulation

Lesson 33

aversion
deficient
deterioration
exaggerate
extinguish
ignoble
instill
morose
poignant
slouch

Lesson 34

affirm
bilious
delicate
extremity
gorge
habitual
lineaments
spacious
stout
unwholesome

Lesson 35

adverse
electorate
implement
impose
malicious
mandate
partisan
propriety
skepticism
undermine

Glossary

A

abstinence *n.* voluntary forbearance especially from indulgence of an appetite or craving [21]
accessible *adj.* open to approach; easily reached [3]
achievement *n.* result gained by effort; accomplishment [16]
adjust *v.* to set right; to fit; to regulate [31]
adverse *adj.* against; not favorable; antagonistic [35]
affirm *v.* to assert; to give testimony; to support by statement [34]
alight *v.* come down from something [21]
alleviate *v.* to make less severe; to lighten as a burden; to remove stress [1]
allocated *v.* measured out; distributed [9]
allusion *n.* indirect reference; hint; implied reference to something familiar [4]
alter *v.* to make different; to modify; to change without loss of identity [10]
altruism *n.* unselfish consideration for others; selflessness [1]
anatomical *adj.* related to the scientific study of structure, either animal or plant [20]
anecdote *n.* a small story, usually entertaining and frequently amusing; a short account [14]
antiquity *n.* ancientness; age; something related to time long past [32]
anxious *adj.* concerned; worried; fretful [28]
apparatus *n.* materials or machinery designed for a function [20]
apparent *adj.* obvious; open to view; clearly seen [27]
arbitrate *v.* to decide or determine; to make a judgment [19]
ascend *v.* to move from lower to higher position; to rise [3]
aspire *v.* to seek a higher goal [22]
audible *adj.* capable of being heard; detectable by ear [23]
aversion *n.* turning away; repugnance; antipathy [33]
awe *n.* fear; dread; amazement; wonder [29]

B

beamed *v.* smiled with joy [26]
beguile *v.* to pass; to while away; to spend [25]
behalf *n.* benefit; interest [9]
belie *v.* to deceive; to tell an untruth; to misrepresent [18]
bestow *v.* to give; to apply; also, to use [1]
bewilderment *n.* state of confusion or disorientation [23]
bilious *adj.* ill-tempered or out of sorts [34]
blight *n.* decline; decay; ruin; withering [17]

C

capable *adj.* competent; fit to perform a task [19]
campaigns *n.* organized efforts to bring about a particular result [9]
celebrated *adj.* distinguished or famous; occasionally, infamous [20]
chafe *v.* to rub; to irritate by rubbing; to heat by friction [3]
chivalrous *adj.* civil; well-bred; courteous [32]
citadel *n.* fortress; stronghold [31]
clamor *n.* outburst of sound; loud cry; noise of discontent [31]
cocked *adj.* turned to one side; tilted [16]
compel *v.* to force; to pressure [4]
composed *v.* made up [13]
concepts *n.* ideas; things conceived in the mind [2]

Glossary

conciliate *v.* to bring together in goodwill; to negotiate; to restore peace [32]
concur *v.* to coincide; to agree; to act together [4]
consisted *v.* composed or made up—usually used with *of* [5]
console *v.* to extend comfort; to smooth over; to end distress [30]
contradictory *adj.* opposing; inconsistent; on the contrary; against the grain [19]
copious *adj.* full of thought, information, or matter [21]
corrupt *adj.* tarnished; evil; rotten [29]
course *n.* direction or movement, as from A to B [10]
crevice *n.* a narrow opening; a crack [15]
cupola *n.* a small structure, usually domed, built on a roof [20]
curious *adj.* strange; rare; unusual [7]

D

dais *n.* raised platform in a hall or large room [16]
dapper *adj.* stylish; modern; neat; trim [30]
daunt *v.* to frighten; to intimidate; to subdue by fear [30]
dearth *n.* lack; scarcity; shortage [14]
defiance *n.* resistance; challenge [15]
deficient *adj.* not adequate; lacking in quality; falling short [33]
define *v.* to outline; to explain or describe; to distinguish [23]
deliberate *v.* to plan carefully and with specific intent [30]
delicate *adj.* fragile; frail [34]
demeanor (demeanour) *n.* behavior toward others: outward manner [21]
deposit *n.* something set aside for safekeeping [9]
derive *v.* to come from a source; to trace the origin of [10]
despairingly *adv.* hopelessly; despondently [15]
detach *v.* to separate from; to remove [23]
deterioration *n.* worsening of a condition [33]
dilapidation *n.* condition of rot or disrepair [17]
dingy *adj.* grimy; smoky; soiled [20]
discernment *n.* perception; recognition; detection [19]
dismal *adj.* gloomy and cheerless [15]
dispel *v.* to do away with; to remove; to get rid of [4]
dispensable *adj.* capable of being or doing without [21]
disposition *n.* a natural tendency or prevailing mood [29]
dissect *v.* to divide into parts; to cut up; also, to analyze [20]
dissolve *v.* to break into parts; to disappear or vanish [10]
diversity *n.* quality or state of having different forms or types [2]
drawl *v.* to speak slowly in a drawn-out manner [30]
dubbed *v.* named or called [2]

E

eclipse *v.* to surpass; to overshadow; to excel [8]
economical *adj.* frugal; thrifty; not wasteful [14]
electorate *v.* voters; constituents [35]
enclaves *n.* distinct territorial, cultural, or social units [2]
endearment *n.* word or act expressing affection [2]
endeavor *v.* to strive; to attempt; to try [25]
endow *v.* to give to; to provide with [10]

entitle *v.* to give a right to; to provide with a title or claim [10]
erected *v.* built [9]
exaggerate *v.* to distort the truth; to increase or exceed the normal; to tell "tall tales" [33]
expectancy *n.* anticipated measure or amount [9]
expedient *n.* a means to an end; that which is advantageous [8]
express *v.* represent in words; convey [13]
extinguish *v.* to put out, as a flame; to abolish; to do away with [33]
extremity *n.* the end of a limb, generally meaning a hand or a foot [34]
exult *v.* to feel overjoyed; to be in high spirits [22]

F

fatigue *n.* weariness from labor or exertion; exhaustion [19]
ferocity *n.* savageness; wildness [8]
firmament *n.* the sky or heavens [11]
flagrant *adj.* conspicuous; obvious; undisguised; deliberate [25]
flanked *adj.* to be situated on both sides of [26]
flawed *adj.* damaged; defective; imperfect [15]
florid *adj.* flushed; reddish [18]
forlorn *adj.* sad and lonely because of isolation or desertion [26]
formative *adj.* capable of being shaped [28]
fragile *adj.* easily broken; weak [13]
frantically *adv.* marked by fast, nervous activity; anxiously [13]
fringe *n.* a border or an edging of hair, strips of material, etc.; trimming [18]
futility *n.* useless act or gesture [5]

G

gallant *adj.* noble; brave; heroic and spirited [32]
garret *n.* attic; part of house immediately under roof [31]
gaunt *adj.* thin and bony; lean [22]
generate *v.* to produce or originate; to manufacture [11]
glisten *v.* to sparkle or shine [18]
gorge *v.* to stuff; to fill; to eat with considerable greed [34]
grave *adj.* somber; dignified [14]
green *n.* grassy park or lawn [16]
grim *adj.* unyielding; stern; harsh and forbidding; fierce [7]
grimy *adj.* deeply soiled; dirty [7]

H

habitual *adj.* automatic; learned through repetition [34]
haphazardly *adv.* in a manner marked by lack of plan, order, or direction [5]
harmonic *adj.* understood; resonant; congenial [16]
headlong *adj.* reckless; without pause for thought [16]
heath *n.* a tract of open wasteland [11]
heir *n.* successor of one who has died; one who inherits property [20]
honorary *adj.* conferred in recognition of achievement or service without the usual obligations [2]
humanity *n.* humankind; all humans collectively [1]
hypothesis *n.* possible solution; tentative theory or explanation [25]

Glossary

I

ignoble *adj.* base; lacking honor; of low birth [33]
illustrious *adj.* famous, usually as a result of outstanding achievement [29]
immolate *v.* to sacrifice [17]
impel *v.* to force; to cause to move; to drive [10]
impending *adj.* soon to occur; approaching [22]
impetuous *adj.* acting with sudden energy, sometimes without thought; rushing with force [3]
impinge *v.* to encroach or invade; to collide; to infringe upon [3]
implement *v.* to bring about; to fulfill an action; to activate what was an idea [35]
impose *v.* to press or force upon; to charge or place upon [35]
imposing *adj.* grand; overpowering; impressive [27]
imprecation *n.* a curse or oath [7]
impulse *n.* force; urge; inclination; tendency; motive [19]
impute *v.* to ascribe; to attribute; to charge or credit [4]
inalienable *adj.* not to be taken away or parted from [10]
incorruptible *adj.* pure and incapable of being corrupted or made sinful [28]
indelible *adj.* permanent; that which cannot be washed away or erased [2]
indifferent *adj.* unaware; insensitive; cold; unresponsive [17]
infernal *adj.* devilish; like a fiend; also, pesky or detestable [8]
infinite *adj.* without limits; unbound; endless [14]
infirmity *n.* feebleness; illness; weakness; shortcoming [22]
ingenuity *n.* inventiveness; cleverness [8]
inhibition *n.* an inner impediment to free activity, expression, or functioning [21]
initiative *n.* introductory action; self-generated beginning [4]
insinuate *v.* to hint indirectly; to imply [4]
instill *v.* to impart or indoctrinate; to add gradually [33]
instinct *n.* natural tendency; unlearned behavior [19]
institute *v.* to set up; to found; to begin; to initiate [10]
intensify *v.* to strengthen; to grow in density and feeling [18]
interlaced *adj.* crossed as if woven together [26]
intervene *v.* to come between; to occur between points [7]
intimacy *n.* closeness; familiarity [25]
intrepid *adj.* courageous; brave; fearless [23]

J

jovial *adj.* hilarious; joyful; gaily spirited [18]
juxtaposing *v.* placing side by side [5]

K

kindling *v.* igniting; lighting [22]
knitted *adj.* contracted into wrinkles [5]

L

laden *adj.* burdened; loaded [20]
lament *v.* to express deep regret; to grieve [15]
laterally *adv.* sideways; sidelong; across [27]
lilting *adj.* rhythmically and with fluctuating pitch [26]
limpid *adj.* clear or transparent [18]

Glossary

lineaments *n.* features, especially on the face [34]
listless *adj.* without energy; sluggish; not spirited or peppy [30]
litter *v.* to scatter rubbish and waste about [20]
lopsided *adj.* lacking in balance, symmetry, or proportion; disproportionately heavy on one side [26]

M

malicious *adj.* wicked; evil; intending to do wrong [35]
malleable *adj.* capable of being bent or shaped; manageable [32]
mandate *n.* an order, instruction, or authority given by constituents [35]
massacre *n.* collective slaughter, usually of human beings [7]
meek *adj.* quiet; shy; unassuming; humble [27]
mellow *v.* to mature; to relax; to soften [30]
mendicant *n.* beggar; one who asks for charity [1]
missionary *adj.* involved in humanitarian or conversion work for a religion [13]
mode *n.* manner; method; custom; form [14]
morose *adj.* sullen; brooding; disagreeably sorrowful [33]
motto *n.* short expression of a guiding principle [2]
muffle *v.* to subdue, usually as sound; also, to cover, conceal, or protect [27]
multiculturalism *n.* relating to, reflecting, or adapted to diverse cultures [2]
mute *adj.* unspeaking; not uttered; silent [19]

N

numbness *n.* lack of emotion or expression [13]

O

oblique *adj.* slanting; not square or straight; indirect [27]
obliterate *v.* to cancel, erase, or wipe out [7]
obsequious *adj.* fawning; subservient; overly patronizing [32]
onslaught *n.* a furious attack [7]
opacity *n.* state of not letting light through; impenetrability [11]

P

pallid *adj.* lacking color; pale [11]
papist *n.* a supporter of the pope (often a disparaging term) [29]
participation *n.* sharing with others; involvement of self [17]
partisan *adj.* exhibiting partiality or loyalty to one cause [35]
patent *adj.* obvious; readily visible or intelligible [2]
perpetual *adj.* uninterrupted; everlasting; indefinite [18]
perpetuation *n.* continuance; maintenance; lack of interruption [28]
perplex *v.* to puzzle; to confuse; to complicate [31]
persecution *n.* harassment; oppression; ill-treatment [8]
personage *n.* a person or people in general [30]
perturbation *n.* disquiet; state of being disturbed or confused [1]
picturesque *adj.* charming; strikingly unusual; suitable for a picture [17]
pique *n.* anger or resentment [17]
podium *n.* speaker's stand; lectern [16]
poignant *adj.* sharp; painfully emotional; piercing; causing deep feeling [33]
polychromatic *adj.* multicolored; many-hued; dazzling [1]

Glossary

posture *n.* the position or bearing of the body whether characteristic or assumed for a special purpose [26]
practical *adj.* related to action rather than theory; sensible; useful [13]
precarious *adj.* not certain; delicately in balance; suggesting danger [14]
precipice *n.* face of a cliff; steep place [22]
precise *adj.* exact; clear; well-defined [11]
preoccupation *n.* state of being engrossed; concern; diversion; distraction of thought [25]
procure *v.* get possession of; acquire [9]
prodigal *adj.* wasteful; thriftless [31]
proffered *v.* presented for acceptance [5]
propriety *n.* sense of what is appropriate or proper [35]
prototype *n.* pattern or model [25]
pulsation *n.* rhythmic throbbing; vibration [23]
pulverize *v.* to reduce to fine powder; to disintegrate; to smash [3]

R

recollect *v.* to remember; to give consideration [4]
recompense *n.* payment; compensation [22]
recount *v.* relate in detail [5]
redeem *v.* to make amends or act to win forgiveness; to save from sin [29]
refugee *adj.* one who flees a country or power to avoid persecution [13]
relate *v.* to narrate; to tell; to recount [25]
relegated *v.* assigned to an appropriate place or situation on the basis of classification or appraisal [21]
relieve *v.* to free from burden; to remove a pressure [14]
reminiscence *n.* the act of recalling things, people, and events [25]
repress *v.* to quell; to restrain heavily; to keep down by force [29]
reproach *n.* reprimand; blame [8]
resolve *n.* determination; firmness of purpose; intent [19]
restraint *n.* control over one's thoughts and actions; lack of freedom [4]
retard *v.* to slow down; to decelerate [11]
retort *n.* a quick reply, as to an accusation; a comeback [4]
reverberate *v.* to echo; to resound, like a series of echoes [3]
revile *v.* to speak against or scold [8]
risers *n.* stage platforms designed to make groups of performers visible [16]
rubicund *adj.* red; ruddy; rosy [30]
ruddy *adj.* red, usually from vigor, exposure, and good health [18]

S

sarcastic *adj.* characterized by bitter, caustic, and often ironic language usually directed against an individual [5]
saunter *v.* to walk idly with no special concern; to amble [3]
savagery *n.* cruelty; brutality [9]
secure *v.* to acquire or obtain [10]
shrew *n.* a scolding, nagging woman [32]
shrill *adj.* sharp and high-pitched, as a shriek; piercing [15]
siege *n.* an attack; an extended assault [32]

site *n.* the planned location of something [9]
skepticism *n.* state of doubt; disbelief; questioning attitude [35]
slink *v.* to move in stealth and silence; to lurk [31]
slouch *v.* to slope; to walk lazily with head and shoulders stooped [33]
sly *adj.* artfully cunning; sneaky [18]
sneer *v.* to jeer, scoff, or scorn, sometimes with laughter, smiles, or facial expressions of contempt [28]
solace *n.* relief from grief or anxiety; state of comfort [1]
solidify *v.* to become solid or compact; to change from liquid to solid state [28]
spacious *adj.* large; roomy [34]
sparse *adj.* limited; not well developed [21]
squabble *n.* a quarrel, sometimes short-lived and of little importance [31]
staid *adj.* serious; sober [3]
staple *n.* a principal commodity; also, that which is most important and necessary [28]
stealthily *adv.* slyly; secretively; furtively [15]
steer *v.* to direct the course of; to pilot [14]
stern *adj.* severe or hard; unrelenting in appearance and manner; humorless [29]
stirring *v.* calling up strong feelings; calling forth as a memory [5]
stocky *adj.* compact, sturdy, and relatively thick in build [26]
stout *adj.* sturdy; solid; substantial [34]
straits *n.* distress; confusion; difficulty [19]
strewn *adj.* spread about; covered over [20]
stringent *adj.* marked by rigor, strictness, or severity especially with regard to rules or standards [21]
strive *v.* to work hard; to labor; to seek a goal energetically [15]
stupefaction *n.* astonishment; amazement [23]
subdue *v.* to crush; to vanquish; to control by force [25]
subjugation *n.* condition of being under the power of another; lack of freedom [1]
subside *v.* to abate; to lessen in intensity; to ebb [31]
succor *n.* help; relief; aid [1]
sundry *adj.* varied; of many kinds; diverse [27]
supremacy *n.* position of power or superiority [28]
susceptible *adj.* especially sensitive; easily affected; as by disease [22]
sustained *adj.* prolonged; continual [21]

T

taint *n.* stain; bare suggestion of sin and corruption; imperfection [29]
tangible *adj.* touchable; evident; having substance; real [27]
tart *adj.* sharp or sarcastic [30]
taunt *v.* to make fun of; to sneer; to jeer at [8]
temperament *n.* mental and physical character of a person [17]
terminal *n.* a passenger station that is central to a considerable area or serves as a junction at any point with other lines [26]
termination *n.* limit; end; final phase [8]
tilted *adj.* moved or shifted so as to lean or incline [26]
tolerable *adj.* capable of being endured [9, 32]
tousled *adj.* disheveled; rumpled [7]
tract *n.* land; region or area without definite boundaries [11]
tranquil *adj.* peaceful; serene; quiet; undisturbed [3]
transitional *adj.* related to change [11]

Glossary

treacherous *adj.* not trustworthy; sneaky; capable of villainy [27]
tribulation *n.* struggle; distress; suffering, frequently from oppression [32]
trustee *n.* one to whom something is entrusted; board member [16]

U

unaccountable *adj.* not capable of explanation; mysterious [31]
unconscious *adj.* unaware; involuntary [14]
undermine *v.* to weaken or ruin gradually another's health or reputation [35]
undulate *v.* to move in a heaving fashion, as in the manner of waves [23]
unification *n.* process of making into a unit or a coherent whole [5]
unspeakable *adj.* too awful to put into words; horrible [13]
unsmirched *adj.* clean; unblemished; untarnished [28]
unwholesome *adj.* not healthful physically, spiritually, or morally [34]
utterly *adj.* totally; fully; completely [7]

V

vagary *n.* odd or eccentric action [22]
vanity *n.* conceit; excess of pride; self-love [28]
vast *adj.* large; huge in bulk; unbounded; immense [11]
vault *n.* a burial chamber; a tomb [15]
venerable *adj.* worthy of reverence and respect [17]
verdure *n.* greenness, especially a garden, grass, or other luxurious vegetation [27]
verge *n.* border; limit; margin; edge [17]
version *n.* form or variant of an original; adaptation [13]
vibration *n.* trembling motion [23]
vie *v.* to attempt; to strive; to compete [29]

W

wan *adj.* pale or sickly; pallid [23]
whoop *n.* exuberant shout [16]